Snows of Yesteryear – A Translator's Story

GW00480830

Snows of Yesteryear–

A Translator's Story

An Autobiography

EWALD OSERS

Lawrence

with every good wish for Christmas + 2008 from Ewald + Mary

Elliott & Thompson
London

Contents

PART ONE

Childhood / page 7
Early Teens / 18
Middle Teens / 24
Pre-war Prague / 37

PART TWO

England / 49
Evesham / 58
Caversham Park / 74

PART THREE

After the War / 81
America and Italy / 99

PART FOUR

Professional Travel and Activities / 115
'I grow old, I grow old…' / 149
'But I have promised to keep…' / 156

Chronology / 163
Complete Bibliography / 167

PART ONE

Chapter One

Childhood

When I was born, on 13 May 1917, I was a subject of His Apostolic Majesty Charles I, by the Grace of God Emperor of Austria, King of Hungary and Bohemia, of Dalmatia, Croatia, Slovenia, Galicia, Lodomeria and Illyria, King of Jerusalem, etc., Archduke of Austria, Grand Duke of Tuscany and Cracow, Duke of Lorraine, of Salzburg, Styria, Carinthia, Carniola and the Bukovina, Great Prince of Transylvania, Margrave of Moravia, Duke of Upper and Lower Silesia, of Modena, Parma, Piacenza and Quastalla, of Auschwitz and Zator, of Těšín, Friuli, Ragusa and Zara, Prince-Count of Habsburg and Tyrol, Kyburg, Gorizia and Gradiska, Prince of Trient and Brixen. Margrave of Upper and Lower Lusatia and in Istria, Count of Hohenems, Feldkirch, Bregenz, Sonnenberg, etc., Lord of Trieste, of Cattaro and in the Wendish Marches, Grand Voyvod of the Voyvodship of Serbia, etc. etc.

A year and a half later, with the surrender of the Central Powers on 11 November 1918, the reign of Charles I (subsequently called Charles the Last) was at an end, as was also my brief period as a subject of the Habsburg monarchy. As I had been born in Prague, I automatically, without any legal proceedings and without any filling of forms, found myself a citizen of the newly created Czechoslovak Republic. Being a small child, I was of course unaware of these momentous historical events – but I do remember that on 28 October 1928, on the tenth anniversary of the new republic, when I was just over 11 years old, I wrote my first poem to celebrate the occasion. It was an absolutely terrible poem, but I still remember its first four lines:

Trommelgewirbel und Paukenschlag,
Soldaten ziehn durch die Strassen von Prag
zu Ehren des zehnjähr'gen Bestandes
des tschechoslowakischen Landes.

The reason why I wrote this poem in German was that we were a German-speaking family. My mother had been born in Linz, in Austria, where her father was a judge. When he was up for promotion to Landesgerichtsrat, apparently the first Jewish judge to reach that level in the Austrian judiciary, it was suggested to him that he change his conspicuously Jewish name of Abeles. Having a sense of humour, he decided to change it to Anders, meaning 'otherwise'. Following his promotion he was transferred to Prague, a step up from Linz. (I have been told by my mother that, when a further promotion to Gerichtspräsident was offered him, this time on condition of baptism, he declined. He had no objection to changing his name, but, though by no means particularly religious, drew the line at abandoning the faith of his ancestors.) Anyway, his move to Prague meant that my mother, then a teenager, entered the Mädchenlyzeum, a German secondary school there, which existed into the 1940s.

My father came from a Prague Jewish family, but, like most men with an upper-middle-class or professional background, had gone to German schools and considered himself as belonging to Prague's German society. He was a member of the Deutsches Haus, a social club, and a member of the Deutscher Theaterverein. He was also a member of Schlaraffia, a club practising a humorous persiflage of medieval knightly society, with its strict mock-medieval ceremonial. The language in Schlaraffia – which had branches in many countries – was German, at least in Prague, and its membership was partly Jewish and partly non-Jewish. I mention this because in the late 1920s or early 1930s the different cultural traditions did not yet integrate a great deal.

My father must have known Czech, but probably spoke it badly; anyway, after the foundation of Czechoslovakia he decided, by then in his early forties, to take Czech lessons in order to acquire a better command of the language of the country he was now a citizen of. As for his Judaism, he was totally assimilated, not religious at all, and only went to the synagogue once a year, out of filial piety, as he said, on his mother's Jahrzeit. My mother often told me that one of his regular sayings was: 'Whether Jew or Christian is irrelevant; one's got to be a good person.' In line with this secularized atmosphere we were not circumcized – a fact that later saved my brother's life – and we had no Bar Mitzvah. My father was a *Direktorstellvertreter*, an assistant manager, at the head office of the *Böhmische Unionbank* – *Česká banka Union* – on Příkopy.

At Christmas we had a big Christmas tree and our presents were laid out underneath it on Christmas Eve. On one occasion, when I was quite small, when the tip of the tree had to be cut off to fit into our room (which was probably about 10 foot high), I remember asking why they had not simply made a hole in the ceiling; surely Dr. Salus (who lived above us) would not have minded. Not until several years later did I first hear about Chanukah. I was never given any 'militaristic' toys; on one occasion when someone gave me a pistol that fired a cork tied on with string, with a popping noise, I was not allowed to have it.

But I remember, especially when I was in bed sick, enjoying those Japanese flowers which, when floated on water, opened out into beautiful colours.

My father died when I was six, and I have very few memories of him – most of what I know is what my mother later told me. But I do remember a few moments. Once – I must have been four or five – I came home from the park crying. Another boy had hit me. I remember my father telling me, rather crossly: 'A boy doesn't cry when another boy hits him; he hits him back.' Another recollection: when I was bending down to do up my shoelaces, my father told me, and showed me, that it was easier to put one's foot on a stool or chair rather than bend down.

My father was one of the first skiers, at a time when this sport was still virtually unknown. Together with two friends, one of them our dentist, Dr Ofner, he would – I think before he got married – go to the *Krkonoše* mountains, where the native population stared in surprise at the antics of those three gentlemen on long wooden boards. I don't think that my own love of skiing is a hereditary feature, but it is probably true that my (rather protective) mother's readiness to let me go skiing while still at school had something to do with her knowledge that this had been a favourite pastime of my father's.

We were on holiday in Mariánské Lázně when my father, on 2 June 1923, died at Bad Nauheim in Germany, where he had been for treatment. He died of a massive heart attack – this was before defibrillators had been invented. His death was at first kept from me. But one day, while I was walking with my governess on the promenade, a stranger came up to us and said: 'Isn't this the little Osers whose father has just died?' My horrified governess rushed me back to the Hotel Metropol, where we were staying, and of course I had to be told then. I have no doubt that this encounter with the thoughtless stranger was more traumatic for me than the news itself.

The law required the appointment of a guardian for me and my brother, or the appointment of two co-guardians. The latter course was chosen in our case, and my mother was one co-guardian, while my father's best friend, a patent lawyer named Schweinburg, was the other. I did not greatly like him.

Over the following years my mother, who visited my father's grave at the Olšany cemetery every Sunday, often took me along with her, telling me about my father on the way there and back, usually by tram. This was probably the most 'quality time' we had together when I was a child, because usually I was in the care of our governess. My mother was a very beautiful woman, with natural fair hair. She had married young – at not quite twenty. My father was eighteen years older than her. They had an exceptionally good marriage and his death, after a little over seven years of marriage, really devastated her. In spite of numerous offers she never remarried.

My paternal grandmother died just before the end of the First World War, leaving me – as I was subsequently told – a substantial amount of money in Imperial War Loans which, of course, with Austria's defeat, became totally worthless. But it was a kind thought of her.

We had a cook and a maid, both of them Czech, of course, though I suspect they understood some German. But my mother spoke Czech to them, in her very broken but evidently serviceable Czech, and so did I. There was, of course, a *domovník*, a concierge, who lived with his family in a kind of semi-basement from where he was able (and perhaps supposed) to keep an eye on who entered the building. During the day the building was open, but the front door was locked by him at 8 or 9 pm, and anyone arriving later had to ring the bell and the concierge or his wife would come and open up. Non-residents were expected to give him or her a tip. In the basement there was an old-fashioned laundry used by the tenants on a roster. I remember that on our 'wash day' an elderly woman, called Anna, who had been employed by my father's mother, would come round and help with the big wash. The place was always full of steam and would probably violate present-day health regulations.

There were other people who came to the house. There was Herr

Stieber, who came to cut my hair and give my mother a pedicure. And there was Fräulein Wilma, a rather pretty (as I thought as a boy) hairdresser who attended to my mother's hair and also manicured her. Each year a *Weissnäherin*, a seamstress, would come to the house during the day, for two weeks, be set up with a treadle sewing machine, and make our shirts and underwear, repair bed and table linen, etc. When I was old enough to wear suits (with short trousers) a tailor came to the house with sample swatches of material, and would measure me for whatever my mother ordered. And a few days later he would come for a fitting. I well remember that, on one such occasion – I must have been about twelve – he informed me in a confidential voice that 'a gentleman wears his equipment in the left trouser leg'. I do not remember when I first bought anything ready-made. These arrangements may sound very feudal from a present-day point of view, but they were then the usual pattern in upper-middle-class families in Central Europe.

Our routine medical and dental care similarly did not require us to leave the house. Although a cousin of my mother's, Siegfried Abeles, was a general practitioner and was frequently consulted over the telephone for minor problems, I was fairly regularly seen by a paediatrist who came to the house. At first this was Dr Bunzl – whom I liked because, prior to examining me, he invariably produced a brightly coloured pastille for me from a little silver box – and later it was Professor Fischl, the head of the Childrens' Hospital – whom I did not like because he preferred the old-fashioned method of listening to my chest by putting his ear against it and his face, several hours after he had shaved in the morning, was rather prickly.

Our dentist was Dr Ofner, a friend of my father's and his former skiing companion, who was by then our tenant on the third floor. I remember that, when I was small, he always, before examining my teeth, let me ride up and down in his dentist's chair.

When I was about five my father engaged a German, or maybe even Prussian, governess for me, a Fräulein Zehle. He had seen her one summer in Mariánské Lázně supervising a group of children at play and had clearly been impressed by her competence. He had, on the spot, given her his card and told her that, if she ever wished to change her employer, she should get in touch with him. I remember very little about her, but the fact that I speak with far less of a Prague-German accent than most of my friends (and that, when I speak English, I have more of a German than a Czech accent) is no doubt due to her.

It should be remembered that a certain knowledge of German was widespread during the first few years of the republic in all classes of Prague's population, largely as a legacy from the Austrian monarchy, and more especially among the men who would have served in the imperial army. I remember that, as a child in the 1920s, I often went shopping with my mother. In shops where she was not known as a regular customer she always started speaking in her broken Czech, whereupon the shop assistants readily switched to German – by no means perfect German, but a lot more fluent and correct than was my mother's Czech.

Where, when, and how, in this bilingual atmosphere, did I learn Czech? The truth is: I really don't know. I certainly spoke Czech to our cook, having probably heard my mother speak to her in her broken *Kuchelböhmisch*. And I suppose in the park I sometimes played marbles, or other games, with Czech-speaking children. But I have absolutely no recollection of any early language acquisition. I do, however, recall one linguistic incident when I was a little boy of maybe five. When I heard my mother, probably talking to the cook or the maid, refer to a young girl as *žába* – clearly her colloquial vocabulary was better than her grammar – I said: 'But mummy, *žába* is a frog, not a girl.' Later, when I was nine or ten, I had Czech lessons from a tutor, a young university student, who came to the house about twice a week.

Living as we did in a town, and moreover in a flat, we never had any pets such as dogs or cats. But I do remember that as a small boy I had a tree-frog – no doubt a misguided present from somebody. This lived in a glass box, on a vestigial branch or twig. The container had air holes and there was a 'feeding trap' with a sliding cover over it. The frog had to be fed regularly with flies. These had to be caught – I was too young to be any good at this, but my governess and I think the maid were kept busy catching flies by hand which, then, still alive, had to be slipped through the feeding trap. I do not remember being particularly fond of this pet frog, and I certainly was not heartbroken when one day it had disappeared from its glass prison. It was later found down the lavatory, drowned – evidently it had somehow escaped and sought out a source of water.

Many years later – I was in my teens by then – we had a pair of lovebirds in a cage. I cannot remember what happened to them, but I do not believe we had them for long.

At the age of six I started school – the elementary school in Vladislavova. Like the other children – after all, Prague was a city with quite a lot of traffic – I was taken there and met again at the end of lessons. I have a vague recollection of some of the children crying the first day or the first few days, but I rather enjoyed it. I clearly remember my first day at school: we each had to stand up and say our names. And I also remember – it was, of course, a coeducational school – that I immediately fell in love with one of the girls, Lucy, with whom I either continued to be in love, or fell in love again (I can't remember which) in my early teens. Sadly she died in New York a few years ago. For our first lesson our teacher brought in a stuffed fox. Had we been country children, we would have immediately recognized the animal, but being town kids only some of us knew what it was, and then probably from picture books or the song *Fuchs, du hast die Gans gestohlen, gib sie wieder her ...*

Like some of my class mates I could more or less read when I started school. I hadn't been formally taught, but I had for some time asked my *Kinderfräulein* – governess is perhaps too grand a title, but she ate with us at table, at least for lunch – what individual letters on shop signs were and what the inscriptions said. So I was able to read and also to write in printed letters. But 'joined-up writing' was something new. Although we were marched off, boys and girls separately, to their toilets during the breaks between lessons I recall that some children occasionally had accidents and the school janitor had to be called in to mop up the floor. I don't remember feeling sorry for those poor embarrassed kids.

By the time I started school my brother Hans (now he calls himself Jan) was two years old, but I don't recall that he played much of a part in my life then – though I do remember being taken to the nursing home, the Sanatorium Gottlieb, to see my new baby brother.

School was only in the mornings, so I must have been taken to the park in the afternoon, my little brother no doubt in his pram. I remember playing marbles with other children – ball games were considered 'too rough'   and I still have a feeling that efforts were made, probably unenforceable, to prevent me from playing with 'undesirable' children, who might have lice or use words I wasn't supposed to know.

We lived very centrally, just behind the National Museum, with a small park – today largely sacrificed to ventilation shafts for the Metro station *Muzeum* – in front of our house. This was a five-floor building that my father had inherited from an aunt of his and which, after his death, was my mother's principal source of income. We had a large flat on the first floor. It was filled with a lot of beautiful things which, even as a child, I appreciated. My father was a keen and serious collector of early Meissen china. In the 1920s, during the inflation in Germany, he acquired a unique princely Meissen service, so 'important' from a collector's point of view that it took several months before he obtained the German government's permit to have it shipped to Czechoslovakia. A large cupboard, set into the wall, was specially built for it in our flat. The service consisted of several hundred pieces, hand-painted with flowers and with a cobalt-blue and gold border to plates and cups. It had to be washed in warm, not hot, water and was brought out for use only on special occasions. Another thing my father collected was clocks, ranging from antique pocket watches to (mostly French) ormolu clocks with figures. I also remember a Flemish tapestry. He was probably less of an expert on paintings than on china and clocks, but we had a putative Claude Lorraine – 'attributed to Claude Lorraine' – two small forest-brook scenes by Samuel Ruisdael, a 'possible' Carl Spitzweg, two landscapes by Ferdinand Georg Waldmüller and others I don't recall. I do, however, remember a small still-life painting with a skull resting on a book: as a young child I was frightened of that picture and never went near it when the light was switched off. Needless to say, all these things were later stolen by the Nazis.

Incidentally, I recall the replacement of our gas light by electric light – I must have been about four – and our first telephone. I even remember the number we then had – 9331.

I also remember emptying the lift's money box with my mother at regular intervals. For the tenants use of the lift was free: they all had a key to it. Outsiders had to drop a 1-Crown coin into it for the lift-cage door to open.

In my childhood horses had almost disappeared from the street scene, the only exception being the heavy dray horses pulling the coal carts. Most buildings and shops in central Prague had coal cellars, with heavy hinged metal lids covering the chutes down which the coal was delivered from the coal carts. And I remember old-fashioned lorries with an external chain drive.

In the winter, 'maroni men', sellers of roasted chestnuts, appeared at major street corners with their braziers. You got ten chestnuts for one Crown, but you usually had to throw one or two bad ones away. Even so, this was a popular and cheap purchase on cold days. The twist of paper with the hot chestnuts kept your fingers warm in your overcoat pocket.

About that time, when I was five or six, I saw a naked girl for the first time in my life. A little girl, on the Císařská louka, an island in the river, where families went to bathe and sunbathe. It would be impossible, with Prague's public statuary and the decorations on its art-nouveau buildings, for any little boy or little girl to grow up without an acquaintance with the anatomy of the opposite sex – but seeing a live naked girl must have been sufficiently different, or I wouldn't have remembered it. (It was to be many years before I saw an adult woman in the nude.)

My childhood holidays, after my father's death, were nearly always spent in Austria, and I have a vivid memory of the elaborate preparations for them. Admittedly there were four of us – my mother, my brother, myself, and our governess – and we would be away for nearly two months. But weeks before our departure huge cabin trunks were standing about our flat, being packed. The day before our departure our 'tame' porter, a Mr Drtina, who had been doing this for the family for many years, arrived at our home, took complete charge of all the heavy luggage, and arranged for it to be consigned to our destination. So that, when our departure day actually arrived, we only had to get a taxi to take us and our hand luggage to the Wilson Station, now the *Hlavní nádraží*. I cannot remember what happened to our heavy trunks when we arrived, nor how the homeward journey was organized – but evidently it worked.

On one of those holidays it was decided that I should learn to swim. The usual practice then was for the learner to be strapped into a harness, with the instructor keeping high and dry at the bathing establishment and holding the learner on a rope and pole, the pole supported on a rail. I am told I screamed and cried, certainly I didn't like these swimming lessons at all. So my mother stopped them and decided she would teach me herself. She got me a swimming belt with about ten brick-shaped pieces of cork strung on two cords, got into the water with me – as all modern swimming instructors do – and taught me to do breast stroke. After a few days she took one of the cork bricks off. Then another, and so on, and in a very short time I was swimming. My mother, though certainly not an athlete, swam well and was also a good tennis player. After all, she was only a little over thirty when I was ten.

On one summer holiday in Austria, in Velden on the Wörthersee, I developed paratyphoid fever – probably, according to the local doctor, from eating an unwashed pear. This was quite a dangerous disease then, I had a temperature of 42°C and, as I was told afterwards, had nightmarish hallucinations about Lilliputians. (I had just read *Gulliver's Travels*.) To make matters even worse, my little brother developed scarlet fever at the same time. The hotel, the *Schlosshotel Velden*, was alarmed – and who can blame them? – but rose brilliantly to the challenge. At the far end of their extensive grounds, which included a number of fish ponds, there was an unoccupied *Fischerhäuschen*, a fisherman's cottage, a small two-storey building. My brother was accommodated on the upper floor, looked after by Tante Bertha, a great-aunt of my father's who lived in Vienna and who invariably turned up whenever there was a family crisis. I myself was on the lower floor, attended by my mother. At the doors stood washbasins filled with lysol, and anyone leaving either the upstairs or the downstairs room had to thoroughly wash their hands in it. My mother and Aunt Bertha were not allowed to go near one another and had to communicate by shouting. The hotel – no doubt for a considerable charge – delivered meals to the fisherman's cottage, but just deposited them outside to avoid a possible spread of infection. We were both very sick, but after some weeks recovered, were declared to be no longer infectious and travelled back to Prague. There, within days of our return, in spite of all elaborate precautions, I developed scarlet fever. (But my brother, fortunately, did not catch my paratyphoid.) I was not nearly so sick with scarlet fever as I had been with paratyphoid; indeed, apart from itching I don't remember anything unpleasant. The only painful thing was that all the books I had read while I had scarlet fever had to be burnt. And our flat had to be fumigated afterwards while we were accommodated in a nearby hotel for a few days.

I had, of course, missed many weeks of schooling but arrangements were made for one of the teachers from my elementary school, a Fräulein Brosch, to come to our house during my convalescence period and coach me in what I had missed. I think I was in the third form at the time.

The school regulations in the First Republic allowed pupils to skip the fifth (the final) year of elementary school and go on to the Gymnasium provided, of course, the pupil passed the secondary school entrance examination. I have a clear memory of my mother inviting the elementary school headmaster, who was a fellow-*Schlaraffe* and hence almost a personal friend, to our house to assess whether I was fit to 'skip' the fifth form. He asked me a few questions and decided that I should go ahead and take the entrance exam. I have no recollection of that exam, but I must have passed effortlessly, and in the autumn of 1927 I entered the *Deutsches Staatsrealgymnasium mit humanistischer Abteilung*.

Early Teens

My secondary school was located, during my first and possibly second year, in Jindřišská. I went there, and back home, unaccompanied, even though it meant crossing the busy *Václavské náměstí*. I don't remember much of my first year at the Gymnasium. Only that, because there were so many of us, we were divided into parallel forms by the alphabet. My name starting with O, I was of course in IB. At the end of the fourth year our ranks thinned out considerably, some pupils switching to commercial schools, so that from the fifth year on, the Quinta, the A and B forms were amalgamated and we found ourselves with many new classmates. Another thing that happened in the Quinta was that we were split into a 'humanistic' and a 'modern' stream, the former taking Classical Greek and the latter English. As I had by then been taking private English lessons, and also because I was a good Latinist, a lot of pressure was brought to bear on me to take Greek. Which I did. I actually quite enjoyed it. For all other lessons, of course – except the by then optional religious instruction which hardly anyone took – we were all together.

As I have just said, I did not regret choosing ancient Greek. Although our Greek master was not such a good teacher as our Latin master, I was attracted to learning a new language and, when we got to reading it, ancient Greek literature fascinated me. Ancient history, on the other hand, did not interest me at all, the Peloponnesian War bored me and Plato's philosophy did not particularly grip me. But Homer enchanted me – especially the lyrical passages in the *Iliad* and *Odyssey*. But also Homer's almost modern psychology. I am thinking, for instance, of the scene when Ulysses as a shipwreck asks for asylum at the court of the Phaetians. In line with ancient custom, he was given hospitality and his hosts tactfully refrained from asking who he was and where he had come from. In the course of the meal the court bard sings about the dangers and adventures that Ulysses had passed – unaware that the hero of his stories is among his audience – and Ulysses, moved, begins to shed tears. (Apparently in antiquity it was quite all right for men to cry.) His well-mannered hosts pretend not to see it and Homer's account of the scene reflects a growing tension among the banqueting company. Finally, Ulysses believes that good manners demand that he introduce himself; he stands up and says: 'I am Ulysses, Peleas's son, who has experienced numerous misfortunes …' It is a fantastic scene.

Our Greek master – he was the headmaster – was, even for his day, rather prudish. Thus, when Homer described a woman (or a goddess) as *bathykolpos*, literally 'deep-bosomed', this was translated as 'high-belted' (*hochgegürtet*) and if she was *kallopygos*, literally 'with beautiful buttocks', this was rendered as 'with a fine figure'. Yet we were by then seventeen or eighteen, even though boys and girls together, and a more literal translation wouldn't have shocked or embarrassed anybody – except, of course, our headmaster.

The bolder ones amongst us sometimes made fun of the headmaster's prudishness. I clearly remember that one of my classmates, a girl, asked to recapitulate what we had read in the previous lesson, naughtily said about one of the numerous lovers of the chief god Zeus: 'Zeus had an affair with her and had made her a child.' The shocked head severely corrected her: 'Adler, when we are speaking of the gods we say: he was fond of her (*zugetan*) and from their love there sprang (*entsprang*) a child.' But the headmaster was a decent man and often shielded students against stricter masters.

This is a good moment to speak of private lessons. I had been receiving tuition in Czech since I was about ten or eleven – a nice young man, a student, I think, by the name of Rozskočil, came to the house once or twice a week. I started English lessons when I was twelve or thirteen. My English teacher – she had probably been recommended to my mother – was a rather eccentric Cornishwoman by name of Trembath and lived on *Na Perštýně*. She had been living and giving lessons in Prague for some years. I have no idea if she knew any Czech or if her pupils were all German speaking. Actually, she couldn't speak German either, but she had a considerable German vocabulary. I know that when the post man rang her bell, she would call out, in English: 'Who's there?' and refuse to open the door until the postman had learned to answer, in English: 'postman'. However, I learned quite a lot from her and actually passed the English Proficiency exam run by the German University in Prague. A few years later – I was by then in my upper teens – I also had French lessons. An elderly Swiss lady from Neuchâtel in Switzerland – she claimed that the best French was spoken there – had been coming to the house as long as I can remember, to give my mother informal

French conversation practice. She came to lunch with the family perhaps every two or three weeks and the conversation was in French.
(However, when I started French I had formal lessons from her, with
declensions, irregular verbs – the lot. But that was not till later.) From
about age eleven I also had piano lessons, indeed I continued with them
for some six years. But because I hardly ever practised I didn't get very
far. Also I soon discovered that I was more interested in music as such
than in the piano. And instead of practising I messed about with piano
scores of operas or also tried to play from orchestral full scores.
However, I did occasionally play chamber music, at my piano teacher's
home, and accompanied my classmate Erich Fitzinger, who had a fine
baritone voice, in some Schubert songs. I also, for a number of years,
went to PT classes at the *Deutscher Turnverein* and on Sunday mornings went to fencing classes – Italian sabre – at the same place.

These private lessons, to which others were subsequently added, were
possible because school was only in the mornings – from 8 am to 1 pm.

My Gymnasium was by then in *Štěpánská*, which was much more
convenient for me: I could walk there in ten minutes. And halfway to
the school, where *V Tůni* ran into *Žitná*, I would stop and wait for Lucy
(whom I still or again loved) to come down the hill and walk with her
to our school. She was now a form below me, not having skipped the
fifth form of the elementary school. Unfortunately she did not recip-
rocate my feelings and instead had a (before very long sexual) relationship with a cousin of mine. But we remained friends.

It was probably on my thirteenth birthday that I was given a bicycle.
I do not think my mother ever felt happy about me riding it. To begin
with, she insisted that I had proper instruction from my PT teacher at
the *Deutscher Turnverein*. In retrospect this was not a bad idea. He
taught me different ways of mounting and dismounting, and he broke
the monotony of riding round and round the gym hall by teaching me
how to replace a valve, how to mend a puncture, and how to replace a
tyre. For a long time, however, I was not allowed to ride my bike in the
city. I had to push it – quite a long way – to the *Stromovka* park in order
to ride it there. When I was a little older I was eventually allowed to ride
it in town, until on one occasion my front wheel got into a tram line –
bicycle tyres then were narrower than nowadays – and I had a bad fall.
I suppose I was lucky not to be run over.

I started skiing at age thirteen. Our school had a *Skiheim* in the
Krkonoše mountains – or, more correctly, two of them, one for boys and

one for girls. Those were dormitories in peasant chalets, very simply but adequately equipped. I don't think I particularly enjoyed my first season: I was very much an awkward beginner and the weather was cold and windy. It was probably not for another two seasons that I became a really passionate – and eventually good – skier. On one or two occasions I went skiing with the *Deutscher Turnverein,* when some of the adults encouraged me to join them on quite difficult tours, such as the *Kozí hřbet* or the steep and difficult run down to Krummhübel on the German side of the mountains. Not until my upper teens did I start skiing with a small group of friends, male and female, in chalets we rented for ourselves.

Puberty and the onset of sexuality are delicate subjects to write about, but to pretend they didn't happen, or that one changed straight from childhood to manhood, would be silly. I behaved no differently from other pubertal boys. In bathing establishments I would look through knot-holes at girls undressing, and I soon discovered that pubertal girls similarly enjoyed looking at (and sometimes asked to be shown) boys' erect penises.

About that time I also had my first date. Gretl, a cheerful girl, full of laughter, lived in *Karlín*. We had arranged to meet at the corner of *Jindřišská* and *Václavské,* in front of Julius Meinl. She was nearly half an hour late, but I waited. We went for a walk in *Riegrovy sady,* the park where Franz Kafka used to walk with his women friends – though at that time I had not read any Kafka. It was all extremely proper and chaste – we did not even hold hands. Several decades later, during which we had lost contact with one another, she wrote to me from Saskatoon, Canada, where she was the Acquisitions Librarian at the university. She had come across my name as the translator of one of the books she had 'acquisitioned' and got my address from the publisher. For something like twenty years – she had by then lost her husband – I phoned her once every year from our winter address in Florida and we had quite a chat. She sounded as cheerful and full of fun as in her teens. She died a few years ago in Canada after a massive stroke.

When I was a young boy my mother also took me to watch top-class tennis and international tennis stars. This was on the *Štvanice,* an island in the river. I remember seeing the famous French 'trio' of Henri Cochet, René Lacoste and Jean Borotra – 'the flying Basque', so called for his spectacular performance at the net. But I also remember those legends of Czech tennis, the brothers Koželuh. The more famous of the two brothers, Karel Koželuh, together with Pavel Macenauer, represented Czechoslovakia in the Davis Cup in the 1920s. (I was told – but did not witness this myself – that at a demonstration game Koželuh displayed his mastery of ball control by asking for chalk circles to be drawn on the far side of the net and he would then hit the ball to drop into those circles.) Later, as a teenager I frequently watched the then top players of Czechoslovakia, Josef Maleček and Roderich Menzel. Although Menzel was a German speaker, he represented Czechoslovakia in the Davis Cup and at other international tennis events. (After the war he played for Germany and also became a successful writer. He is still alive – now 94.) And Maleček was not only a top tennis player, but also captained Czechoslovakia's ice-hockey team. I would often, as a teenager, stand (well wrapped up) on the unheated tribunes, also on the Štvanice, to watch Czechoslovakia's ice-hockey team which was even then of high international standard and in 1933 won the European championship.

Another sport I was fond of watching in my early teens was football, and I was a frequent visitor to the grounds both of Sparta and Slavia. On several occasions I saw the legendary goal-keeper František Plánička in action. But I had no particular loyalty to either of the two major clubs. On one occasion, I remember, I also went to the Sparta grounds to watch the long-distance runner Paavo Nurmi, but I don't remember attending many athletic events.

It was also during my early teens that I began to go to the theatre, to the opera, and perhaps to my first concerts. As for the theatre, there were school performances of the classics, which we were encouraged to attend. The first opera I was taken to, by my Uncle Fritz, my mother's younger brother, who was an opera singer in Germany and frequently visited us in Prague, was Weber's *Der Freischütz*. A good opera for a child or near-child: it has a simple story of a good guy and a bad guy, magic bullets, and other supernatural stuff. And the music is enjoyable and uncomplicated. I soon became an opera lover, and by the time I was in my upper teens had seen and heard most of the usual operatic repertoire.

The first four years of my secondary school, the *Unterstufe* of the Gymnasium, left little impact on my memory. I loved Latin and became rather good at it. I quite enjoyed German literature, physics and chemistry, but was rather bored by history and geography. I don't think I did any homework during my early years at the Gymnasium, but even so I managed to get school reports with only 'very good' and 'good' grades. Perhaps it should be said that there was absolutely no anti-Semitism at our school. Several of the masters were Jewish and, in my form, just about half the pupils. The non-Jewish masters came mostly from the Sudetenland, but there the Henlein Party, the 'Home-into-the-Reich' party, did not really gain much strength until after Hitler's rise to power in Germany in 1933. There was one religious Jew in our form, the son of a Prague rabbi, who did not write on Saturday – yes, we had a six-day school week – and we therefore knew that there would be no written tests on Saturdays. (But I don't think he was observant enough not to take the tram to travel to school.) Prague Judaism was very liberal and assimilated. I never saw an orthodox Jew in the streets of Prague. It was only during holidays in the Bohemian spas, in Mariánské Lázně or Karlovy Vary, that I saw Eastern Jews, in felt hats and long caftans, and bearded. It has to be admitted that the assimilated Prague Jews, none of whom spoke Yiddish any longer, regarded these eastern Jews with contempt and dislike – not suspecting that two decades later they would share the same terrible fate with them.

Middle Teens

It seems to me in retrospect that the years between fifteen and eighteen were the most important formative years in my life. They were the years when I began to see the world around me, when I became interested in social and political issues, when I was avidly reading – Freud, Marx, Wilhelm Reich, some of the positivist philosophers – when I became a regular theatre and concert goer, and when I formed my most important relationships. And probably also the years when I fell lastingly in love with Prague. It is difficult now to recall the sequence of these more or less simultaneous processes.

I don't know how, with my various private lessons, I found time to stroll about Prague – but stroll about the city I did. On one heroic occasion I even climbed the tower of St. Vitus Cathedral – several hundred steps in semidarkness, up to the enormous bells and to a breath-taking view of the city. I loved the labyrinth of passages through the old houses with their courtyards in the old city and fancied myself quite an expert on them. Some of them – exactly as Jaroslav Seifert has described – were the hangouts of prostitutes who, if you declined their solicitations, would call out angry vulgarisms about what you could do with your penis. If I had enough time I would go to the Seminary Garden, especially when the cherry trees were in blossom, or to the park that climbs up the slope of Petřín Hill.

About that time I was invited to a party by a second or third cousin of mine, whom I didn't really like. But our mothers were friends and it would have been difficult to refuse. He went to a different school, I think the *Realschule* in Mikulandská, and I hardly knew any of his guests. After the meal the lights were turned out in the large sitting room for a group snogging party. At that point Willy Schenk, a boy from my school whom I only knew slightly then, and I walked out into the next room – maybe because we had no snogging partners, but really, I think, because the whole business didn't appeal to us. Instead we played table tennis. It was the beginning of a lasting and close friendship – we were 'best friends' until years later, in England after the war, he died of a brain tumor. Willy was a brilliantly gifted young man. We would meet several times a week to go for long walks, discussing music, literature, and politics. On one occasion, when we were together in Austria, we climbed the 3,507 m *Zuckerhütl*, one of Austria's highest mountains – with a professional guide, of course, who roped us up on the tricky bits. It was a wonderful experience and we both enjoyed it hugely. But for a long time I was in utter disgrace with Willy's over-protective parents for having 'enticed' their son into such a dangerous exploit. This was not my only mountaineering experience of those days. But I always had a guide for anything that was in the least dangerous, and I never did any real rock-climbing.

Another sporting exploit, when I was fifteen or sixteen and on an unsupervised holiday at Staré splavy in northern Bohemia, was that, together with a classmate, Liz, I swam across the Mácha Lake. I got into trouble afterwards, and rightly so, because we had not told anyone what we were about to do and there could have been an accident.

By then Hitler had come to power in Germany. One result of this was that many of us students in the upper forms of our Gymnasium gravitated towards the political Left. (This became even more marked after the outbreak of the Spanish Civil War in 1936. But I will deal with that later.) All that needs to be said at this point is that, when an aggressively anti-Soviet play, *Tovarishch*, was staged at the German Theatre in Prague, a few of us youngsters decided to whistle and boo at one particular point – when, after the rape of a young girl, one character says: 'What else can you expect of a Bolshevik?' The police had clearly been tipped off to the possibility of a demonstration and there was a plain-clothes detective in the standing places behind the stalls. And, although I can't whistle, not even to save my life, he pounced on me and arrested me. Unfortunately, my mother was in the theatre too, somewhere in the front stalls, and with the house lights going up during the fracas, she saw me being marched off and rushed out herself. This was both lucky and unlucky for me – unlucky because everybody at school, including the masters and the head, knew of the incident by the following morning, but lucky because of my mother's connections. She immediately got hold of the Deputy Director of the theatre, who was in the house, to intervene and get me released on the promise that a strict eye would be kept on me. I remember that after the performance – or maybe the performance was still continuing – she and I were sitting in the Café Alfa with our hurriedly summoned lawyer, really almost a family friend, who undertook, no doubt at some financial cost, to see that my name was kept out of the papers. Strangely enough, this was the only time in my life that I was arrested.

There was one occasion, however, when I might have easily been arrested. Before a general election I was tearing down a poster of the Czech party that was the equivalent of the Nazi Party in Germany. Out of nowhere a policeman appeared, demanding what I was doing: tearing down election posters was a punishable offence. I showed him the poster I had just pulled down. 'That's all right,' he said; 'but don't let yourself be caught again!'

In those days there was no such thing as sex instruction in school. But in the Septima, the seventh form, when we were around seventeen, the school doctor came one day and spoke to the boys – I am not sure what the girls were doing during that time – about sex. As far as I remember, this was not about the physiology of sex, with which we were all, at least theoretically, familiar, but about the dangers of sex, in other words about venereal diseases. The instruction ended with all of us boys being made to promise, 'on our honour', that we would always, at all times, carry a condom in our wallet, because – and I remember these words accurately – 'the morning does not know what the evening may bring.' I rather think that, by then, I was doing that anyway.

At the end of my eighth year at the Gymnasium I took my Matura, the school-leaving exam that entitled one to enter a university. There was a possibility under the rules – very rarely made use of – for school-leavers to write and submit a Matura Essay. I don't quite know why, possibly because a cousin of mine in Vienna had written one on Richard Wagner, I decided to write one too. This was on Ancient Greek Music. It listed a lot of quotations on music from classical Greek literature, described what was known of Greek instruments, and dealt at some length with Aristotle's writings on tone intervals and scales. I had done quite a lot of reading on the subject, but my work, alas, is lost to posterity. The exam involved several written papers and an oral examination before a commission that included the headmaster and a ministry inspector. As far as I remember, I had no difficulty with the written papers. During my oral exam I recall naughtily and provocatively – in response to a question on 'parasitism and symbiosis' – launching into an account of protective symbiotic bacteria in the vagina, but the embarrassed headmaster stopped me. Anyway, I passed 'with distinction'. That was a few days after my eighteenth birthday.

In retrospect I think that our Gymnasium was above the average of secondary schools. It certainly is a fact that some students who did not gain entry to it – their first choice – then went to a German Gymnasium in Smíchov.

While I was at school, the names of two of its famous alumni were frequently invoked – Max Brod and Franz Werfel – and occasionally they would appear in person, as honoured guests, at school events. Among my contemporaries quite a few made a name for themselves, mainly after emigrating to the West – Walter Süsskind, the conductor and composer, who was two forms above me and who set one of my poetry translations to music while still at school; Alexander Kafka, my classmate, who became a Director and later a Trustee of the International Monetary Fund; my classmate and good friend Ota Gregor (then Gans), who became a famous gastroenterologist and a few years ago received the prestigious Purkyně Prize; Karel Lewit, an internationally recognized back-pain specialist, at eighty-five still consulting three afternoons a week and – even more impressive – still a downhill skier; Walter Bor (formerly Buchbinder), who became an internationally famous architect and town planner, awarded the CBE, but now sadly dead; Herbert Lom (originally Kuchacevich von Schluderpacher), who made a tremendous career as a stage and film actor, and Kurt Mautner, who, under the name of Marcello Cortis, was a successful baritone who sang at La Scala in Milan and at the Aix-en-Provence festival. Lenka Reinerová, 'the last German-writing author in Prague', was a class-mate for the first four years of my secondary school. She has been a hugely successful writer and, not long ago, was made an Honorary citizen of Prague.

And yet, the teaching at our school was by no means outstanding and the methods were rather old-fashioned. Would those of us who have achieved something in their lives have done so if they had gone to a different school? One of my classmates, Franz Wiesmeyer (later, in England, George Whitman, a gifted violinist who occasionally gave recitals), decided one day that the wooden forms we sat on were rather uncomfortable. Having established that there was nothing in the school rules against pupils using cushions, he had an elegant dark-brown leather cushion made, perhaps 3 or 4 cm thick, with a handle, so that it could be carried just like a brief case. This he brought to school with him day after day. It earned him a reputation for eccentricity, but he wasn't eccentric at all – he just had a sense of humour and there was, of course, an element of provocation and anti-school-establishment in it.

We also had some odd, or near-eccentric, characters among the teaching staff. Our Latin master, Professor Sturm, who was also our form master, was an excellent classical scholar but had what even in the 1930s was a very old-fashioned view of linguistics. He didn't believe that languages were living and developing organisms. To him Latin was the language of Cicero. Authors before him 'did not yet know Latin properly' and the authors of the Augustan age – whom, of course, we also read – 'no longer knew Latin properly'. Being a devout Catholic, it pained him greatly that the Latin of the liturgy was not his classical Latin. I distinctly remember him observing one day that the liturgical *Miserere nobis* 'should really be *Misereat te nostri*'. But odd or not, I learned a lot of Latin from him. Our history master, Loebl, was a great supporter of the *DFC*, the *Deutscher Fussball Club*, in Prague, a club that very rarely won its matches. But it was certainly better to be examined by him after a victorious match than after a defeat. When he tested you on dates – he was rather fond of doing that – and you came up with a wrong date, he would say: '*Gibts gar nicht*' – doesn't exist at all. Our PT master, Süss, was really a drill sergeant at heart. An enormous amount of time was spent, or wasted, on making us form ranks of two, changing into ranks of three, forming single and double files, about-turning, and so on. But even so it was quite a popular subject: there was no homework to be done and there were no tests. Our philosophy master, Kampe, supported Hitler's demand for the incorporation of the Sudeten region into Germany. But when Hitler in March 1939 invaded the rest of Czechoslovakia – having previously declared the Sudetenland to be his 'last territorial demand' – Kampe, disillusioned, committed suicide.

The teacher who influenced me most, and probably also a lot of my classmates and friends, was Oskar Kohn (who later changed his name to Kosta). He was our Czech master, even though his mastery of that language was a little suspect. He made no secret of the fact that his political views were to the Left and was therefore viewed by his colleagues on the staff with some suspicion, though they probably liked him as a person. Some of us attended private classes at his home. It is difficult to define their subject – they were an integrated presentation of literature, art, sociology and politics. And he was very good at it. He certainly made me see literature, art, architecture, and culture generally, as springing from the socio-political soil. This may sound like a Marxist interpretation, but it was not. Oskar – who out of school encouraged us to call him by his first name and say '*Du*' to him – was not a theoretician but genuinely enjoyed culture and enjoyed conveying this enjoyment to his young friends, whom he was fond of referring to as 'my young people'. I have often disagreed and argued with him, especially in later life, in England, but I have always felt a fondness and a debt of gratitude to him. It was also he who led our trips to Italy and did much to make us understand and appreciate what we saw there.

By then I was a frequent theatre, opera and concert goer. I remember in particular one star-studded performance of Schiller's *Don Carlos* with Moissi as the Marquess Posa, Ernst Deutsch as Don Carlos, Albert Bassermann as King Philip, and Tilla Durieux as Princess Eboli. I also went to many concert rehearsals, especially when Bruno Walter was conducting. This was tolerated rather than officially permitted, but if one pretended to be a music student the attendants would let one in. I remember feeling a kind of moral obligation to acquaint myself with contemporary music. I loved Mahler and Richard Strauss then and I still love both of them today. But although I conscientiously went to performances of Schoenberg, and on one occasion attended nearly every performance of a Prague Festival of Contemporary Music, I have to admit that I do not find myself in tune with it. As for Schoenberg, I can take *Verklärte Nacht* and perhaps the *Gurrelieder*, but that is about all.

I also remember visiting Alois Hába at his home: he was then a professor at the Music Conservatoire and a protagonist of quarter-tone and sixth-tone music. He had a quarter-tone piano and a sixth-tone instrument at his flat and demonstrated some of his music to me. His kind of mini-interval music never really caught on.

The most important event of those years was the beginning of my relationship with Edith. I think we knew one another some time before, the way people within the same Prague German circle knew each other. Both our mothers were widows – in fact, they lost their husbands the same year – and both our fathers had been in the same bank. I remember having been interested in her for some time and having told Willy Schenk that I would very much like – as the phrase then was – 'to go' with her. No hope, he told me, she's going with Kurt – a boy I knew. However, when we were both on the same group trip to Italy, in the summer of 1935 – for me and a few others it was a *Maturareise* – we fell in love with each other in Venice. What better place is there for falling in love? From Venice we went to Rome and I remember that there, one evening in the darkened Colosseum, we kissed quite a bit – much to her subsequent remorse as this was the birthday of her boyfriend Kurt. Back in Prague she first tended to regard our Italian kisses as a holiday romance, but before long we came together. And from that moment we were inseparable. I would meet her as she came out of school and travel with her on the No.11 tram to see her home – she was living just below the *Letná* – and take the tram back to the Museum. My family, whom I made thereby late for lunch, didn't seem to mind at all. Edith and I went together to the theatre and to concerts, and together discovered Gustav Mahler. We went together to the evening lectures by Max Deri, a wonderful art historian who was a refugee from Hitler's Germany, who greatly widened our understanding and appreciation of art and architecture. In short, we did nearly everything together. The customary pattern of behaviour between young lovers then was rather different from today: although we enjoyed very satisfying sex play, always with our clothes on, we did not have penetrative sex. I am almost surprised in retrospect at the matter-of-fact way we treated our being what today is called an item. Even more surprisingly, our mothers quite expected us to turn up together whenever one of us was to meet their mother. We went skiing together, not always, but sometimes, staying at the same chalet.

It was about then, and undoubtedly triggered by this happy relationship, that I started to write poetry seriously. (When I looked at some of these German poems recently, in connection with sending my papers to the Památník národního písemnictví, the Czech national literary archive, I was astonished at the maturity of some of it.) I used to show my poems to Fritz Bruegel, the Austrian poet who came to Prague after the failure of the 1934 socialist rebellion in Austria, in which he was personally involved. His frank and intelligent criticism was exceedingly useful to me. Fritz Bruegel, with whom I remained in touch during the war, when he too was in England, is, in my judgement, still not adequately appreciated as an early-20th century German poet.

As for my relationship with Edith, I have no doubt that it helped us both to mature. I believe it marked the beginning of my adulthood.

I have two memories of Prague's musical life that may be worth recording, as few witnesses are still living. The first concerns the death of the conductor Eugen Pollak. After a career in Germany and America he returned to his native Prague in 1933 to conduct a performance of *Fidelio*. I was up 'in the gods', in the Standing Gallery and thus had an excellent view into the orchestra pit. Very soon after the opening of Act One I noticed, and heard, Pollak swaying and bumping into his desk. With his right arm he gestured towards the ground-tier boxes, where Georg Széll, the opera chief of the theatre, was sitting – but at that time no one seemed to understand the meaning of his gestures. Then suddenly, just before the opening of the quartet, he knocked his desk over completely and collapsed into the arms of the *Konzertmeister*. Other players rushed to his assistance while the *Konzertmeister* leaped on to the conductor's rostrum and with his violin bow beat time. I saw Széll rushing out of his box and a moment later appearing in the orchestra pit. In a few strides he mounted the rostrum and was just in time, without the score which must have been flung somewhere to the ground, to give the cue for the opening of the great Act One quartet, *Mir ist so wunderbar*... The soloists on the stage must have seen what had happened, but they were professionals and the quartet was sung perfectly, if perhaps a little more tremulously than usual.

When the curtain fell on Act One the Deputy Director of the theatre appeared at the footlights to announce that Eugen Pollak had died off-stage and that, as a tribute to him, the performance would be suspended. The following morning the papers announced: 'Eugen Pollak comes home to die'.

My other experience is less sad, but perhaps more incredible. I often went to the final rehearsals of concerts; these were open to the public. On the occasion in question Alexander von Zemlinsky was conducting Beethoven's *Missa Solemnis*. At one point he tapped his desk, interrupting the play, and turned around to the audience. 'I feel that somebody is watching me through opera glasses. Would you please put them away?' And someone in the audience did. It should be said that Zemlinsky was terribly shortsighted, that he wore thick glasses, and that even if he had turned around – which he did not – he could not have seen the culprit. It was an amazing display of an artist's extreme sensitivity.

Equally important as my relationship with Edith was my experience of the Italian Renaissance – not only on that 1935 trip but also on several subsequent ones. (Indeed, Italy was my wife's and my preferred holiday venue many years later, after the war. I believe that I have been to Italy seventeen times – and not just lazing on some beach, but absorbing and – if this is not too grand a word – identifying with what to me is the European tradition.) Intellectually, I suppose, I accept the role of ancient Greece, of Greek philosophy, Greek drama, and Homer. But neither ancient Greece nor the impressive legacy of Rome and of Latin literature had on me the direct mind-blowing impact of Renaissance Italy. I may of course be quite wrong with my assessment, not being a cultural historian, but this is what I feel and what I have felt from my first contact with Italy – a sense of meeting myself. Not only in the works of art, but in such instinctive, non-deliberate things as the proportions of buildings, the location of country houses and ancient hill-top villages, the layout of Renaissance gardens. This may be very unscholaly – but the sight of these things makes me feel happy, unreasonably so, just as the sights of Prague, whenever I revisit my native city, make me feel happy. But whereas a sense of being at home is natural enough in one's birthplace, it surely has an enhanced significance in places like Verona, Vicenza, Lucca, Siena, Urbino, Ascoli Piceno, and many others. Venice, I think, is different: there I do not feel the same identification; instead I just marvel at it as I do at Granada or Avignon. This is why I could never live happily outside Europe. I am, for better or worse, a European.

After my *Matura* I registered – 'immatriculated' was the official term – at the German University in Prague to study chemistry, with physics as my secondary subject. I had been interested in chemistry for some time, and having graduated from a German secondary school the German University in Prague seemed the natural progression. In point of fact, since my Gymnasium was a state school, my graduation would have entitled me, had I wished to do so, to enter the Czech university, Charles University. Having learned my chemistry and physics in German, studying at the Czech university would have been a lot more difficult to start with – but, in 1935, this was never a real option. On the advice of a friend of the family, Professor John, the head of the Institute of Hygiene, I simultaneously entered the German Technical University for the first year, my first two semesters. In retrospect I am doubtful whether this taught me more chemistry than I would have learned by being merely, like everybody else, at the university. But I remember my professor there, Hüttig, who had gained some fame for inventing a special type of crucible. He was obsessed with neat laboratory practice – maybe not a bad thing for beginners. No bottles were allowed on the lab desk: acids had to be put back immediately after use on the shelves above the desk and solvents in the cupboard below the desk. The desk itself had to be covered at the beginning of each day with a large sheet of white filter paper, or perhaps white blotting paper, and Hüttig would walk around to see what spots, if any, his students had left on them.

At the university, the head of the department, Waldschmitt-Leitz, who had recently arrived from Germany – not a Jewish refugee at all – was engaged, interestingly enough, on a research project for the German army. He was trying to find a way to make army bread look bigger without using more flour or any other ingredient. He had baking tins and would measure the height of his loaves. He discovered, if I remember correctly, that the addition of some copper salts made the bread rise higher and thus, from the same amount of starting material, produce a larger (or a larger-seeming) loaf. It was perfectly legal for senior university staff to do privately funded research – but I thought even then that his particular line of research was significant. The Nazis were getting ready to deceive their own troops.

I also remember a girl – she was a German Jewish refugee – coming to our department in Prague to continue her research into rancidity products. As she progressively concentrated her material, its smell became increasingly overpowering, and eventually she had to be confined to a small laboratory room of her own.

Despite this dual study from the autumn of 1935 until June 1936 I seem to have had enough free time to spend many hours with Edith, to continue my private English lessons, to play tennis at least once a week, to go to concerts and to the theatre, and to attend the art history course of Dr Deri. Indeed, I added additional classes: from 1935 to 1938, when I left Prague, I attended a history of culture class with Oskar Kosta, who had been one of my teachers at the Gymnasium, a music class with Professor Kestenberg, a refugee from Germany, where he had been high up in the musical education system (this class only for a few months), another music class with Hermann Grab (likewise only for a few months), and an occasional set of art lectures at the home of Oskar Baum. I also went to lectures and regularly attended the meetings of the *Blok* group of left-wing writers. I felt, and probably was, very much alive.

From about the age of sixteen I attended, as was then the custom, regular *Tanzstunden* – literally 'dancing lessons', but in fact dancing parties for teenagers. One dressed up, boys in dinner jacket, girls in splendid taffeta dresses, and there was a professional band playing. The girls were usually chaperoned by their mothers, who sat somewhere outside having a *Kaffeeklatsch*. Before I started going to these events my mother, anxious that I should cut a good figure, had sent me to a few real dancing lessons. I vaguely remember an exceedingly buxom and over-perfumed instructress, who kept urging me to hold her closer. I quite enjoyed those dances, except that my mother made me promise that I would dance, at least once, with the daughters of her friends – no matter how plain they were.

At the end of the school year our Gymnasium always held what was called an *Akademie* in the big Lucerna Hall. Technically, the *Oktava*, the final form was in charge of the organization. There were all kinds of 'displays' – the gymnasts performed impressive 'pyramids', using illuminated staffs or clubs, there was at least one musical item by the school orchestra, and there was, in my year, even a jazz band with me at the piano. I remember that one of the tunes we played was the then popular *Parlami d'amore, Mariù*. We had two outstanding saxophonists and we were a great success. The performance traditionally concluded with a formal *Vortanz*, an opening dance, for which we were rehearsed by a professional for many weeks. Ours was a Polonaise, danced to Chopin's famous *Polonaise in A-major*. I had the honour of being in the first pair – not so much an honour, perhaps, but because the socially ambitious mother of my partner Hedy – a very nice girl, still living in Toronto, as far as I know – would only let her partner me if I ensured that we were the opening couple. Somehow I managed to arrange this. After the *Vortanz* the general dancing began and went on for hours.

Some time in the mid-thirties my mother decided, mainly on the advice of her legal and financial advisers, to have our house pulled down and replaced by a modern building. Our 'old house', dating from the turn of the century, contained six or seven flats, but it was in many respects old-fashioned and the plot on which it stood, in a prime location in central Prague, was probably worth more than the building. A modern block could contain about twice that number of flats, and since the yield from their rents was my mother's principal source of income, the project made sense. I remember that a few of her friends thought that this was a risky decision at a time of political uncertainty, but most people at that time were reasonably optimistic and the economic arguments were compelling. The architect chosen for our 'new house', a well-known architect called Paul Eisler, was 'modern' without being outrageously avant-garde. (He also had a very pretty niece, but that was not a factor in our choice.)

The building next to ours on Čelakovského sady – our house was a corner building – was a small hotel of dubious reputation, *Hotel Neptun*. Building regulations required that the plans of new buildings had to be

agreed by neighbours. And the *Hotel Neptun* made its consent depend-
ent on our undertaking to pay for an extra storey to be added to the
hotel – otherwise, they argued, the discrepancy in height would spoil
the skyline. My mother was advised to accept their conditions. The
hotel's clientele may not have been quite what we would have wished in
our immediate neighbourhood, but evidently it was numerous enough
to fill another floor. Today the former hotel, with 'our' top floor, is a
block of flats.

For a little over nine months, therefore, while the old house was
demolished and the new one built, we had to live elsewhere – not too
far away, in a rather smaller flat on Tyršová.

Management of a much larger block of flats would be a bigger job,
and my mother therefore arranged with a cousin of hers, who was interested in renting one of the flats in the building for his family, that, for a
reduced rent he would see to the entire business side. Which he did very
efficiently. He lived on the fifth floor, while our flat was on the third. I
used to envy him a little, because from the fifth floor upwards you could
from the balconies, over the roofs of the 'New' and the 'Old Town', see
the Hradčany Castle.

With the outbreak of the Spanish Civil War, and especially once the
involvement of Nazi Germany was obvious, I identified increasingly
with the political Left. I wore a badge with a three-pointed star on my
lapel, the symbol of the 'United Front'. In France, under the growing
threat from Germany, the Communist and the Socialist Party had just
formed the 'United Front', and this seemed to us a necessity also in
Czechoslovakia in order to stave off the Right-wing threat from without and within. Although, unlike many of my friends, I did not join the
Communist Party – there were too many aspects of its philosophy to
keep me from doing so – I was persuaded to join the *Kostufra*, the
Communist Student Fraction, which was not part of, or subject to, the
Party. My 'cell leader' was Katya, whom I have not seen since 1938, she
died in 2001. I was made the *Kulturreferent* of my cell, the person
responsible for cultural matters, but do not remember that this involved
any particular duties. I do, however, remember that I repeatedly dis-
agreed with official Communist policy and therefore was accused of
Trotskyism – the favourite label for non-orthodox views, even though
I had never read a word of Trotsky's writings or knew anything about
Trotskyism.

On the twentieth anniversary of the Soviet Union thousands of blue cards – the size of postcards – were distributed with S.K. Neumann's verses:

Vám poděkování a lásku vám,
kéž zněly by jak zvony –
Už ne já já sám, už nás jsou miliony…

[*Thanks and love to you,*
may they ring out like bells –
no longer I alone, now we are millions…]

I don't remember how it came about, but I was asked to provide a German translation for a German version of these anniversary cards. Which I did, though anonymously. I suppose it was an honour to be asked – I was only twenty at the time, and there were several better known German translators of Czech poetry in Prague, and most of them with left-wing leanings. Anyway, I was quite proud of this early literary and political achievement.

One political action I remember was a fortnight's camping in the summer of 1937 in the hills of northwestern Bohemia, in the by then predominantly Nazi-oriented Sudetenland. There were perhaps two dozen of us, young men and women, and we called ourselves *Freie Jugend*. I remember that, on the way to our chosen location, we marched through Karlsbad (Karlovy Vary), demonstratively singing socialist songs – but the truth is that no one really took any notice of us. Otherwise the camp was no different from other camps: there was nothing particularly political about it. We slept in tents, lit a big campfire in the evening, roasted potatoes in the hot ashes, and bathed in the nearby river. I quite enjoyed it, largely because – Edith had some time before broken with me – of a girl called Kitty. (She was later deported by the Nazis, but survived the concentration camp and returned to Prague. I learned this from the lists that were published after the war. I have not met her since that summer of 1937.)

Pre-war Prague

A lot is being written and talked about the exciting cultural scene in Prague during the last few years before the war, about the intermingling of three traditions – a Czech one, a German one and a Jewish one. Some of these flashbacks are, I think, tinged with wishful thinking, seen through rose-coloured spectacles. These three traditions certainly existed, coexisted, in Prague, and some of us were making very deliberate efforts to achieve an interweaving.

It is difficult to generalize. But on the whole my impression is that in the generation of my parents there was little integration between the Czech and German cultures in Prague. German speakers, whether Jews or Gentiles, went to the German Theatre and to German social clubs, while Czech speakers went to the National Theatre and to Czech associations. German-speaking families subscribed to the *Prager Tagblatt*, *Bohemia*, or *Prager Presse*, while Czech families took Czech papers. I don't think these cultures were at all antagonistic; they just did not integrate much. Yes, I do remember that as a child I occasionally, but very rarely, had other children shout at me '*Žide*' or '*němčoure*', but this happened so rarely as to have been in no way traumatic.

There were, of course, notable exceptions. I remember that President T. G. Masaryk, probably the most enlightened of all politicians in Czechoslovakia, made a point, on 28 October, the National Day, when special gala performances were staged in all theatres, of attending the first act of whatever was given at the National Theatre and then turning up, for the second or a later act, at the German Theatre. No more than a gesture, perhaps, but an important one. Max Brod, a German writer (and a graduate of my Gymnasium), translated the operas of Smetana and Janáček into German. Franz Kafka, who, contrary to general belief, spoke Czech fluently, though he never wrote in Czech and even wrote his letters to Milena Jesenská in German, belonged for many years to the Czech-speaking *Klub mladých* and there took part in its debates. Pavel Eisner and Oto Babler, probably the only Prague writers and poets who were equally at home in both languages, translated poetry both ways. But consistent efforts for integration probably only began with my generation – quite possibly also as a response to the external threat.

I am not sure that there were in fact three cultural traditions: I don't think there was a distinct Jewish tradition in Prague, at least not in my time. There were Jewish writers who wrote in German, like Franz Kafka, Max Brod, Franz Werfel and others, and there were Jewish writers who wrote in Czech, like Karel Poláček. And although Max Brod in an early novel, *Reubeni*, used Jewish themes – just as the non-Jewish Gustav Meyrinck used them in his *Golem* – I question whether they in any sense represented a specifically Jewish tradition. I would say that whatever elements of a Jewish cultural tradition there may have been had long become fused into the literary tradition written in the one language or the other.

We, the young generation, deliberately involved ourselves in this integration process. Unlike the generation of my parents, it was a matter of course for me, as a student, to attend performances at the National Theatre, and perhaps even more so at the Liberated Theatre of Voskovec and Werich, and the E.F. Burian Theatre, while of course continuing to go to the German Theatre. The Liberated Theatre was then almost a cult venue for the younger generation. Its political humour was directed against the Establishment and its songs, by Jaroslav Ježek, were sung and whistled everywhere.

About that time I began to concern myself intensively with contemporary Czech and Slovak poetry: I translated it into German and had my translations frequently published in the Sunday cultural supplement of *Prager Presse* – under the pseudonym Walter Hart. On one or two occasions my translations appeared in the Prague *Volksillustrierte*. Some of them also appeared in the Moscow German periodicals *Das Wort* and *Internationale Literatur*. Two of my own poems also appeared in *Prager Tagblatt*. Some of my translations of socially committed poems were also performed by German *Sprechchor* [spoken choir] groups: this was then a popular form of Agitprop art.

Although I had no particular acting talent, I belonged to a student dramatic group called *Deutsche Studentenbühne*. And we deliberately tried to make contact and perhaps collaborate with Czech student theatrical groups. I very clearly remember our first joint meeting. The chairman of our Czech partners was called Pavel Tigrid. Contrary to the calumnies of the totalitarian regime, that he changed his name from Schönfeld to Tigrid for opportunist reasons when, after the war, he converted to Catholicism, I can testify that for his literary and cultural activities he was called Tigrid even before the war and right through the war, when I worked with him in England on editing the Anglo-Czechoslovak cultural periodical *Review-41* (until *Review-47*). Sadly, he died in July 2003.

Even more deliberate were my efforts to establish contacts with Czech poets and writers. At the suggestion of Bedřich Václavek – who was later executed by the Nazis for resistance activity – I joined the left-wing writers' group *Blok*, where I made friends with the (I believe still underrated) poet František Nechvátal and where, at meetings, I saw many of the giants of Czech and Slovak literature such as Ivan Olbracht, Petr Jilemnický and others, though I did not know them personally. In the group I was one of only three German-writing members, and I was also the youngest. In *Blok* it did not matter if one wrote in a language other than Czech. Some of my own poems and my translations into German were published several times in the group's quarterly *U*, as indeed were Óndra Lysohorsky's poems written in his Lachian dialect. (I shall return later to my friendship with Lysohorsky.) The meetings of *Blok* were held in the Metro café on Národní, or across the street in what is now the Café Louvre.

I think that my mother was quite proud to see my poetry and translations in print, even though she did not share – and perhaps did not understand – my political stance that was frequently expressed in them.

My contacts with Czech poets, needless to say, were not governed by their politics. Even though I then believed in the social mission of poetry, I soon realized that emotionally I was much closer to the subjective lyrical poetry of František Halas, and that even with the socially engaged poets, such as S.K. Neumann and Josef Hora, I was much more in tune with their quiet, melodical, non-political poetry. So I began to translate Halas's poetry into German and to visit him at the editorial office of his *Rozhledy* in what was then Marshal Foch Avenue and is now Vinohradská. I remember the unfailing courtesy with which he always welcomed me and the way in which he, the famous poet, treated me, an unknown student, as an equal.

At the beginning of September 1938, before my departure for England, I went to say goodbye to him. He asked me to send him occasional reports on cultural, mainly literary, events in England. I gladly

promised to do so and asked him for a journalist's card. But those did
not exist in *Rozhledy*, which had no foreign correspondents. Halas
picked up a sheet of notepaper with his journal's letterhead, carefully
pressed his editorial rubber-stamp on it, and signed it. 'Write on it whatever you like. And don't forget to put a photograph on it. To make it
look genuine.' Then he smiled: 'It's not going to help you anyway. No
one knows *Rozhledy* in England.' He was right. It did not help me. But
after seventy years, in the course of which I moved so often and so often
threw out old rubbish, my 'journalistic card' signed by Halas still lies in
the bottom drawer of my writing desk. A few years ago I exhibited it at
a Halas event in Kunštát in Moravia.

My last meeting with Josef Hora was even more moving and certainly more dramatic. I went to say goodbye to him at the *Melantrich* office
on *Václavské náměstí*. The situation in Czechoslovakia in September
1938 was already very tense and loudspeakers were just being mounted on the lamp-posts in the square for the event of an air raid. Technical
equipment, of course, has to be tested. I was already on the other side
when suddenly – evidently the work of an educated engineer – from the
loudspeakers came the beginning of Hora's recently published *Song to
the Native Land*:

> *My country, tried a hundred times,*
> *how often*
> *did you see strangers' hands*
> *tear chunks from your dowry…*

I recognized the text, turned on the spot, raced across the square and
up the stairs, and burst into Hora's office. 'Quick, open the window!' I
panted. He did so just in time to hear the conclusion of his poem:

> *And so we go,*
> *the dead, the living, the unborn,*
> *endless generations:*
> *from the storm clouds over the world*
> *you rise up with us,*
> *island of happiness,*
> *our unending life,*
> *on which we must grow and blossom,*
> *and keep watch.*

He was moved. We were both moved, standing by the open window. I never saw him again.

That my love of Czech poetry endured, and endures to this day, was due mainly to Halas and Hora – and, after the war, to Jaroslav Seifert. I have always regretted that I never knew Vítězslav Nezval, that magician of Czech poetry, personally.

I have often been asked – in interviews and at cocktail parties – whether translating poetry is not 'terribly difficult'. Quite honestly, I have never really known what the question meant or how I was to answer it. Difficult in what way? Like doing long division? Or hitting a target at 100 metres? Or skiing the Kandahar run? From my school days I remember Ovid's statement in his autobiography *Quidquid temptabam scribere versus erat* [Whatever I tried to write turned into a verse] and from later reading I knew Alexander Pope's 'I lisped in numbers, for the numbers came.' It would, of course, be absurd and presumptuous to compare myself to those two poetic giants – and yet, a similar mechanism must have been at work when I translated poetry. Without any conscious effort a translated line – sometimes the opening line, more often the final line – would stand, ready, in my mind. Of course, translating a poem is, objectively, more difficult than translating a business letter, but I have often found translating prose, for instance Thomas Bernhard or Martin Heidegger, a lot more difficult than translating poems. It would be foolish to put on a show of false modesty – having translated hundreds of poems, and having had these translations published, and occasionally rewarded with prizes, I believe that I do have some natural gift or knack for translating poetry. There is no merit to it, no more than running 100 metres in under 10 seconds.

Another frequently asked question concerns my attitude to translation theory or (the fashionable term) translatology. I quite enjoy reading articles on translation theory, so long as they are not above my head – which they frequently are. But I don't believe that translation theory has ever helped me translate. I well remember – it was in Montreal in 1977 – putting this question, about the practical usefulness of theory, to the famous translation theorist James Holmes, himself a translator of Dutch poetry, who sadly died a number years ago. 'Whether or not translation theory helps you translate is entirely beside the point,' James told me in front of an audience of perhaps a hundred; 'like any other scholarly pursuit, translation theory is a quest for the truth. Usefulness has nothing to do with it.'

In retrospect it seems to me that, in spite of my enthusiasm for Czech poetry and for the *Liberated Theatre*, and in spite of my becoming a member of *Blok*, I did not integrate with Czech society on a personal plane. I had no Czech friends then, I never had a Czech girl friend. One or two of my friends studied at the Czech university, but if we happened to meet we spoke German together. One of these, Fred Turnovský, who was also studying chemistry, on one occasion explained the Czech chemical terminology to me while we were walking in the street. (Some fifty years later I met him at a UNESCO-sponsored conference in Washington, DC, which he attended as the official New Zealand delegate. By then he had an OBE and later he received the Order of New Zealand. Sadly he is no longer alive.) On another occasion, when I attended a party at the house of Oskar Morawetz (who after the war became a famous composer and conductor in Canada, with his works performed all over the world) many of those present danced a Czech Beseda – which at the time struck me as a deliberate attempt to identify with the Czech tradition – but, as far as I remember, the conversation was in German. But then, with my background of German schools, how could I have found a Czech contemporary?

(Not until fifty years later, when I was visiting Prague more regularly for literary events and conferences, did I make new, genuinely Czech, friends. More surprisingly, though, my brother and I – who had spoken German together until I left Czechoslovakia at age twenty, when he was sixteen – started speaking Czech together after the war and are doing so to this day, except when in the company of German-only speakers, when we are both in our eighties. Similarly, when I met my old friend Ota Gregor in Prague we also spoke Czech together. This is no doubt an instinctive reaction to what the Germans did to us, and our families, during the war and has nothing to do with any linguistic integration.)

I have to say a few words about Óndra Lysohorsky. I was, about 1937, looking for a synthesis of lyrical poetry and social message – both in my own poetry and in the poems I chose for translation. I had found a few poems by Halas and Hora that seemed to meet that criterion, which I translated. Some of these were read, or chorally recited – a popular Left-wing art form at the time – at political meetings and similar events. But then one day, in the *Prager Tagblatt* I read the translation (by Rudolf

Fuchs) of a poem by Lysohorsky. It turned me on immediately. There, I felt, may be a poet who is doing just what I am trying to do. I went out and bought Lysohorsky's recently published book, *Spiwajuco piaść* [*The Singing Fist*]. Critical reaction to this book had been voluminous, well beyond the usual. A few critics, notably the famous F. X. Šalda, hailed him as a major talent and defended his use of what Lysohorsky claimed to be the native speech of the common people in the Ostrava area. Others, possibly the majority, accused him of inventing a language, of being deliberately gimmicky, and argued that his poetry, if written in standard Czech, would be no more than mediocre. I translated some six or eight of his poems into German and sent them to him, not knowing if he even knew German. Almost at once I received an answer from him, in absolutely perfect educated German (I learned later that he had taken his doctor's degree at a German university with a dissertation on Rainer Maria Rilke). This was not the miner's son who emerged from his poetry – though a miner's son he certainly was. Anyway, his response was enthusiastic, he thought that I had really got into his poetry, and he urged me to translate more. There was a chance, he said, of a major Swiss publisher being interested in bringing out a volume of his poetry in German translation.

When T.G. Masaryk died in 1937, teachers – Lysohorsky taught at a Bratislava Gymnasium – were offered greatly reduced train tickets to come to Prague for his funeral. So Lysohorsky suggested we meet that day in Prague – which we did. We got on extremely well, and an intensive collaboration began between us at that point. I soon had a volume of German translations ready, and, had it not been for the political upheavals in 1938/39, it would have been published by Oprecht in Switzerland. In fact, my German translations appeared several decades later in a scholarly work on Lysohorsky, published by Monash University in Australia. (I resumed my work on Lysohorsky after the war, translating his poetry into English and had a substantial volume published by Jonathan Cape in England and by Grossman in the USA.) On one occasion, when Lysohorsky had a reading in Brno, I went to attend it. After his reading we sat in the famous literary *Kavárna Avion* – Lysohorsky, Jiří Taufer, Taufer's brother, the famous Roman Jakobson and myself. Jakobson was not the severe scholar one might imagine, but was full of fun, telling amusing stories.

By 1937 my life at the German University had become very unpleasant. I was the only Jew in my laboratory and if I turned my back or went out for a moment, one of my Nazi 'colleagues' had either turned off my Bunsen burner or poured something into my experiments. On more than one occasion I found my laboratory bench covered with a large poster: *Nur der studiert, wenn alles marschiert* [He alone is studying when everyone is marching]. There was only one of these students, who was almost a friend; he, too, had studied the first year simultaneously at the university and the Technical High School and we had been walking together from the one building to the other. One day he took me aside and said: 'Look, I support Hitler's claim to the Sudetenland. But I absolutely disagree with his anti-Semitism. I have been trying to protect you as much as I could. But I can't do much more – my father is the mayor of Karlsbad.' This really clinched my decision. I would stick it out until June 1938, which would mean that I would have completed my six *Pflichtsemester*, my mandatory semesters. After that I would be expected to start work on my doctoral dissertation. But, I argued, I would do that abroad and submit my dissertation in Prague to get my degree.

Perhaps it is of some interest that the lecture theatre in which, day after day for the first two semesters, I attended lectures on Experimental Physics was the same theatre in which, some twenty years earlier, Einstein had taught during his professorship in Prague.

Several of my former classmates were studying medicine at the German University and I used to visit them occasionally, during free periods, in the dissection rooms. I remember that the sight of the corpses, some of them dismembered, did not put me off at all, possibly because they had been drained of all blood and looked more like waxwork figures than human bodies. Indeed, despite the odour of formaldehyde, we sometimes ate our sandwiches there.

About that time Count Coudenhove-Kalergi's ideas on Pan-Europeanism – his book had recently appeared – caused a good deal of interest and discussion in Prague intellectual circles.

In March 1938 Hitler invaded Austria. I have a clear recollection of my mother, my brother and me sitting in our sitting room, listening to the radio, which brought a series of news flashes, chiefly the Austrian government's instruction to its army and police 'not to offer any resistance to the German troops that may be entering the country'. In point of fact, the overwhelming majority of Austrians cheered and welcomed the German troops. We realized that this was a bad day for Europe.

Some time in 1937 Edith ended our relationship. This was a terrible and unexpected blow to me. There was no one else – somehow, she felt, she had run out of commitment. But we remained, and still are, good friends.

Before long I had a new girl friend, Ruth – a very pretty girl and a passionate Zionist. This was a very different relationship from that with Edith – much less emotionally involved, far less intellectual, but a lot more sexual. We would go to a cinema at the bottom of *Václavské náměstí*, almost next-door to the Koruna, where, in the privacy of a box at the back, we would pet. Occasionally, when her parents were out in the evening, she would invite me to their flat on Revoluční, where her father, a lawyer, also had his office. On one occasion, when we went on some excursion with a group of young people, we actually shared a room for the night, but even then – such was the force of convention, or perhaps of our fear – we refrained, or more correctly: shied away, from real intercourse.

I did not share Ruth's Zionism and indeed often argued against it. I tried to convince her that there would be no Jewish question and no need for Zionism once a just socialist society was established. I was to be proved terribly wrong. The Jews who emigrated to Palestine mostly survived – though not, unfortunately, Ruth – while most of those who did not emigrate perished in the Holocaust.

Before leaving Czechoslovakia I remember going on a two or three-day hike to the Šumava with Willy Schenk and an English friend of his, Donald Baron, who was staying with him. This was after the Anschluss of Austria but before the Munich agreement. I remember that, just as we were getting to the Třístoleční mountain in the southern part of the Šumava, we saw German frontier guards replacing the former triangular frontier post – Germany-Austria-Czechoslovakia – with a new two-sided one: Germany-Czechoslovakia.

For a young man of military age to leave the country in 1938 was not easy. Nor was it easy to enter England unless one had proof of sufficient means so as not to become a charge on the public purse. However, sending money out of Czechoslovakia was not allowed except with a special permit from the Czechoslovak National Bank. But I was lucky. My immediate boss, Dozent Heller, a Jew, was a personal friend of Professor Jaroslav Heyrovský of the Czech university. Heyrovský was a famous man, he had invented the polarograph and, for that, had received the

Nobel Prize, the only Czech scientist ever to do so. Heller said he would speak to Heyrovský and made an appointment for me. Heyrovský, who had never seen me before, was charming. He there and then dictated a letter to the Czechoslovak National Bank to the effect that it would be in the interest of Czechoslovak science if I were enabled to study abroad. Then he gave me a personal letter of introduction to a Mr Henry Terry, a fellow student of his at University College London and by then a member of the teaching staff there. It would be no exaggeration to say that I owe my life to Professor Heyrovský.

By mid-1938 it was obvious that the pessimists had been right about our new house and my mother began to consider selling it with a view to possible emigration. (Admittedly the same would have been the case if we had still been in our old house.) Since, strictly speaking, under our father's Will, my mother owned half the property and my brother and I one-quarter each, and as I was leaving the country, I had to supply a power of attorney for my mother. And as under pre-war Czechoslovak law a person came of age at twenty-one, I had to be declared 'of age' by the Prague District Court on Karlovo náměstí, a sham-medieval building with a big tower. I remember going there with my mother, no doubt by prior appointment, but the whole business was totally unimpressive and only took a few minutes. Our house was sold to Walter, an armaments firm that a year later collaborated with the Nazi occupiers. This circumstance, together with the fact that the sale took place during what postwar law designated as the 'period of increased threat', and that it was sold for a price well below its real value, was to help us sixty years later with restitution proceedings.

In the early summer of 1938 I flew to London on a brief visit to arrange for my studies at University College. Both Mr Terry and Charles Goodeve (later Sir Charles) were cordial and welcoming – a recommendation from Heyrovský carried some weight. I was taken to the head of the department, Christopher Ingold (later Sir Christopher), who agreed that my six semesters in Prague were the equivalent of a BSc course, and although I didn't have a BSc I would be given all the facilities of a postgraduate student. I formally enrolled for the autumn term and flew back to Prague.

The summer of 1938 saw our last family holiday. We went to Starý Smokovec in the High Tatra. By pure accident the family of an old friend of mine – even a very, very distant cousin – Käte, also spent the summer there. And naturally, although we stayed at different hotels, we went mountain walking together, on one occasion white-water rafting on the Dunajec, and also occasionally going out dancing in the evening. And we experienced a dramatic mountain rescue adventure together. Käte was an experienced mountaineer and, like myself, had once climbed the *Zuckerhütl*. A few days previously we – Käte, my younger brother and myself – had been going on a mild climb with a guide. He seemed to think we were experienced enough to go on a climb, which he told us about, without the need for a guide. We would climb up to a ridge – not a difficult climb at all going up, but not suitable for going back the same way. The only dangerous bit, the guide explained, came just beyond the ridge, where there was a fairly sheer rock-face. However, there was a steel rope fixed to the rock, held by steel hooks every few yards, so, if we held on to that with our left hand, we'd be all right.

When we got to the ridge, somewhat out of breath from the climb, we had a nasty surprise. The steel rope had been torn from the rock-face, probably by a rock fall, and was dangling uselessly in a huge loop. I suppose, being the oldest of the three of us, I felt rather responsible. We couldn't go back the way we had come, and to go on without the safety rope would have been too dangerous. The good thing was that from where we were – now sitting – we had a good view far down. So when, after a while, a group of tiny figures appeared, perhaps a little over a mile away and far below us, we yelled in unison, in German and Slovak: '*Wir brauchen einen Führer! Potrebujeme vôdca!*' and also tried to convey our need by gestures. Amazingly, the people understood and made reassuring signs.

I don't remember how long we had to wait, certainly at least an hour. But eventually a mountain guide – or possibly two, I can't remember – arrived with a rope, roped us up and took us across the dangerous passage. And so we descended, to find our respective parents in considerable anxiety about our late return. Anyway, it was a memorable experience, and if I ever have to get stuck on a mountain again I couldn't wish for pleasanter company.

At the end of the summer I got ready to leave for England. By then the situation was very tense – this was just a few weeks before Munich – and the officials at Prague airport were exceedingly unpleasant. First they didn't like the 'w' in my first name – there was no such letter in the Czech alphabet, they informed me (even though one of the best known Czech poets, Jiří Wolker, was spelled with a 'W'. Unfortunately I did not have the presence of mind to say this to them at the time). One of them then started systematically to strip me. I wasn't particularly worried, I wasn't taking anything out of the country that was forbidden, I was only a little concerned that the plane might leave without me. When they didn't find anything on me they began to go through my wallet. I remember one of them opening a condom sachet and shaking it out into his palm. I suppose I could have hidden a diamond in it. But he put it back again and turned to the two letters of introduction that I had with me. Taking letters out of the country, he informed me, was an offence against the postal regulations: *zkrácení poštovného*, depriving the state of the postage. I calmly offered to pay them the postage and tried to convince them that these were letters of introduction to be handed over in person. In the end they let me go. They probably never had any intention of detaining me, and maybe not even the authority to do so, they just enjoyed their little piece of chicanery. My mother, in the seeing-off enclosure, had been getting very alarmed when all the other passengers had long boarded the KLM plane and I didn't emerge from the customs house until a long time later.

I was not to see Prague again for twenty-seven years.

PART TWO

———

England

When I arrived in England in September 1938 I was not really in the receptive frame of mind of a tourist open to new impressions. I was about to start work at University College London, in a new environment, with new colleagues, and in a language in which I may have been reasonably fluent but whose chemical vocabulary would be unfamiliar to me. And, of course, I was worried about the political situation.

At least I did not have to worry about accommodation. Three friends of mine – Paul Eisler, Magda Starkenstein and Erna Salus – were staying in South Hampstead, in Glenilla Road, and they had managed to get me a room in the house immediately next door to them. So at least I wouldn't be lonely in my spare time. It soon turned out that there was going to be no spare time. My three friends were deeply involved in putting the case of Czechoslovakia before the British public. And within two or three days I found myself roped in. On my own – the others were busy elsewhere – I would address public meetings and rallies on the Czech-German situation inside Czechoslovakia and on the issue of the Sudetenland which had by then been claimed by Hitler for Germany. I was simply instructed – through Paul who organized it all – to be at a certain London Underground station at a certain time in the late afternoon or evening, and someone would meet me there. It worked perfectly, and most of the time I had no idea where I actually was. The meetings were organized by such bodies as the Peace Pledge Union, local Labour Party branches, and others. On one occasion I found myself standing on a wooden platform in the street, under a large red flag and with a London bobby standing right in front of me, busily taking notes.

Even more memorable in retrospect was an invitation I had to Oxford – train fare paid – to have lunch with a group of people and tell them about Czechoslovakia and the Sudeten situation. Only much later was it explained to me that the people I had spoken to were the Fellows of All Souls, the intellectual élite of England. They were perfectly charming, they treated me as an equal, and the lunch was excellent.

I also remember watching an anti-appeasement demonstration in Trafalgar Square, when the mounted police used their horses' rears to push the – entirely peaceful – demonstrators out of their way.

At that time I also thought I might help the Czechoslovak cause by interesting some of England's leading poets in the idea of producing an anthology of contemporary Czech poetry; I was quite ready to provide them with literal translations and give them any other help. I first called on John Lehmann at the office of the Hogarth Press, the publishing house run by Leonard and Virginia Woolf, then on Stephen Spender, who suggested I saw Christopher Isherwood. All three professed sympathy for the idea, but were too busy with other things – and in Isherwood's case with preparations for his 'evacuation' to America. It was a few years before I was able to revive the idea successfully.

My colleagues in the chemistry department of University College couldn't have been nicer or more welcoming. They totally refuted the myth of English insularity. I shared a small laboratory with Barry Whitefoot, a cheerful lad from 'up North', with a Lancashire accent. My supervisor, Christopher (Kit) Wilson, was not only friendly, but before long invited me to his home to have dinner with his family. Barry wet-nursed me, introducing me to the practices of the department, and to other research students on the same floor. He explained that the 4 pm break was a ritual, absence from which was excusable only if one was in the middle of a very delicate experiment. Otherwise one turned up at the tea club. A ludicrously small weekly charge entitled one to a cup of tea (or possibly more than one) plus a cake bought by the baker's dozen from the United Dairy across the road. Very soon after my arrival a man from the ground floor (physical chemistry) appeared, inviting me to join their Seven Seas Club which did not yet have a member from Czechoslovakia. When – I suspect from my conversation with Barry – my colleagues learned that I was a keen skier, they organized a group visit, with me as their non-paying guest, to a skiing display at Earls Court. They encouraged me to come to college dances. They introduced me to some of the undergraduate girl students, one of whom, Mary, later became my wife. (After more than sixty years we are still together.) There were a few non-English research students in the department, notably a Spaniard (perhaps he would describe himself as a Catalan) by the name of Eduardo de Salas. There was also a Dr Wassermann, the son of the inventor of the syphilis test named after him. I also made friends with a research student from the physical chemistry department, Len Wiseman, who later was my best man when I got married.

I soon discovered that my chemical training differed considerably from that of my English colleagues. The training in Prague had been on the lines of the German school, with emphasis on laboratory skills rather than on theory. My manipulative skills were, I think, superior, but my mathematical background could not compare to theirs. All in all though, I couldn't have landed among a nicer bunch of people.

University College London, in Gower Street, presents a classical Grecian façade to the street, but the wing that contained the chemistry department, and several other blocks within the extensive compound, was more modern, probably built between the wars. The whole atmosphere couldn't have been more different from what I was used to in Prague. Straight away I was given a key to a side-door entrance that led straight to the chemistry department. I marvelled at the trust this implied: I could have got in during the night and walked off with all kinds of valuable equipment. Or I could have vandalized the building. But no, I was trustworthy, even though no one had known me for more than a few days.

There were two 'refectories', or canteens, an Upper and a Lower one. Naturally, one tended to sit with one's friends if they happened to be there at the time, but there was an easy camaraderie and strangers would join you at your table and talk to you. I remember being slightly taken aback when a young girl student, whom I didn't know but who told me she was a Pole, asked me if I would sign a petition to the effect that women students should not be made to take exams when they had their period, because they might then perform below their best. Needless to say, I signed. But it was not a subject you would have discussed with a stranger back in Prague. I thought this English openness – even though she was Polish – wonderful and refreshing. I was astonished to discover that there was a tennis court within the complex of the college, where students, by previous booking, could play, as well as a number of squash courts – a game I hadn't known before. It was not until several years later, when I was working for the BBC, that I took the game up myself.

There was a traditional, though basically friendly, feud between UCL and King's College, and students would mount expeditions to steal each other's mascots. I must confess that I thought this a little childish and, besides, I didn't feel that as a foreigner I should get involved.

During that first year in England I continued for a while to write German poetry – some of these poems have appeared in Czech translation (by Zlata Kufnerová) in *Anamnéza*. I also wrote a short story, *Encounter*, the only story I ever wrote. It was never published – I never offered it to anyone – and perhaps it wasn't much good.

I also conducted a coded correspondence with Bedřich Václavek, who was then hoping to get out of Czechoslovakia. He had sent me a copy of a small dictionary of which he had another copy, and we, rather laboriously, corresponded by sending each other what looked like scholarly lists of references – one number followed by a comma and another number. The first number was the page in our dictionary and the second was the word, reading down the column from the top. It was the only 'secret activity' I ever engaged in. Václavek's intentions, however, came to nothing. The Communist Party instructed him to stay in Czechoslovakia and work against the Nazis underground, which he did under the assumed name of Hrdina. Sadly he was caught and executed.

It was later that year that I met and began to walk out with my future wife, Mary. This was a turning point in my life.

Needless to say, my happiness was marred by my anxieties about the political development. I remember clearly that, either during the Munich conference or on the day of Chamberlain's return, Käte – who was likewise studying in England then – and I were hanging about a Black and White milkbar at the corner of Piccadilly Circus and New Coventry Street, watching the ticker tape come out of a teleprinter and following the development of the situation.

As a result of Professor Heyrovský's letter the Czechoslovak National Bank in Prague had authorized the transfer of a monthly sum from my mother to me. I don't remember how much it was – it certainly was a very modest amount – but I recall opening a bank account at the Swiss Cottage branch of the National Provincial Bank with a deposit of exactly £2.

Soon after my arrival in South Hampstead I was approached (I don't remember how this came about) by a group of Left-wing poets, headed by John Manifold, and asked to join them. I did so, but very soon left the group again when they explained to me that, once a just socialist society was established, there would no longer be a place for love poetry or any personal poetry generally. All personal problems would disappear in that collective bliss. I think they really believed that. Nevertheless John Manifold later became a well known poet.

Mary has always been astonished at the way I was keeping in touch with my school friends. When we were walking about London I was forever running into friends from school – and her perception was that all of them had sat either next to me or in front of me or behind me. Naturally a lot of my Jewish friends had by then emigrated, many of them to London, but I do not believe that this shared exile – which we then hardly felt to be exile – explains it all. There was, I think, a strong bond between us while we were still at school, something more than being just classmates, in most cases real friendship and in all cases a strong ésprit de corps. 'Telling' on a classmate was absolutely unthinkable, even when one was, as sometimes happened, unjustly punished. There was also a curious ethos between boys and girls, one that I am told is not necessarily found in English coeducational schools. It was a brother-sister relationship, anything more would have been felt to be incestuous. Boys found their girl friends a form or two below them, and girls looked to higher forms for their boy friends. Maybe this was a subconscious acceptance of the pattern of bourgeois society, where husbands were almost invariably older than their wives. This bond of friendship, which survived the war, was by no means confined only to Jewish fellow refugees: I remember contacting my non-Jewish classmate Erich Fitzinger immediately after the war and meeting him in Austria several times. Our friendship was entirely unclouded by the fact that he had been a soldier – a very reluctant one – in the German army.

At any rate, we have kept up our friendship over the years, meeting at least once a year, though sadly our little band of brothers (and sisters) has now shrunk. And although we sometimes inevitably look back to (mostly comical) incidents from our school days, these are 'contemporary' friendships, not based, as school friendships so often are, only on a shared teenage past.

There were two other lodgers at 19 Glenilla Road, one a medical student called Jim Mitchell, and the other a young man in some business;

I have forgotten his name. We had our breakfast together and, though we did not exactly become friends, they were pleasant and helpful.

I spent some time exploring the possibilities of getting visas for my mother and brother, queuing at the Czechoslovak Trust Fund and making inquiries at the consulates of South American countries. Meanwhile, my mother's uncle, Professor Petschek, a distinguished lawyer from Vienna, who had been enabled with his family to enter the United States through the intervention of Supreme Court Justice Felix Frankfurter, was making efforts to get my mother and brother into America. Unfortunately none of these efforts was successful.

Just before Christmas 1938 I received an invitation from an unknown person to spend Christmas, along with a party of refugees, in Eastbourne. Our host, whom we hardly ever saw, was an elderly gentleman, evidently of some affluence, who was the Master of the local Freemasons' Lodge. His was a big house just behind the seafront and we were treated and fed like lords. Most of my fellow guests were refugees from Germany and Austria. The weather was fine, we went for enjoyable walks – I remember walking up to Beachy Head – and on one occasion we had a treasure hunt. I was also relieved, by a German countess with a famous name, of my by then rather irksome virginity. Last year I saw her obituary in the paper: she had died at the ripe old age of ninety-seven.

In the spring of 1939 my mother came over to England for a brief visit of three days. She left a Persian lamb coat, as well as a diamond ring and a diamond brooch with me. That was the last time I saw her.

In view of the enormous increase in street crime in London – our women friends will no longer travel alone by Underground in the evening, when the carriages are more than half-empty – it may be worth while recording an (in itself trivial) experience. One evening – it was after dark and the streets in my South Hampstead neighbourhood were empty – a young woman asked me if I knew a street she was looking for. It so happened that I did and I offered to walk her there. It seemed the most normal thing in the world – for her to ask me and for me to take her there – and I am sure that neither of us even thought of the possibility of mugging, assault or rape. Those were the days, now sadly gone, of our innocence.

Before that academic year was at an end, on 15 March 1939, the Germans invaded Czechoslovakia. One of the less important consequences of

Hitler's action, but one that was important to me, was that it meant the immediate end of my mother's monthly transfers of money to me. On the morning after the Nazi invasion, before I even had time to reflect what it would mean to me personally, the head of the department, Professor Ingold, summoned me to his office. After a few words of sympathy he stated in a businesslike manner: 'From today you're not paying any tuition fees. And I have given instructions to the stores, and to Mr Nelson, the glassblower, that you are to be given anything you need free of charge.' This was a wonderful gesture, a perfect example of the behaviour of an English gentleman – but, of course, I still had to live. I had to pay my landlady, I had to buy some food, I still had to eat out occasionally. It dawned on me that I would have to look out for a job.

It was Jim Mitchell, the medical student in my bed-and-breakfast place, who drew my attention to an advertisement in *The Times*. The BBC was looking for German translators and announcers. I had nothing to lose and therefore applied. Subsequently I learned that there had been some 4,000 replies to that advertisement. I presented myself at Broadcasting House at an appointed date and took the translation test. I must have done rather well in it because soon I was invited to take an announcer test. I knew from the start that I was bound to fail. My German had a distinct Prague flavour, whereas what the BBC wanted for its propaganda broadcasts was a Prussian voice. I was later told that Stefan Zweig had been their advisor for this selection. A few days later I received my rejection.

The situation was getting tenser, trenches were being dug in London's parks. One afternoon a stranger addressed me in the street in South Hampstead, in German, suggesting that I help fill sandbags at the Hampstead Hospital. This seemed a very reasonable request and for many hours that evening, and again the following morning, I shovelled sand into sacks and helped stack them around the entrance and the ground-floor windows of the hospital.

The college meanwhile was preparing to evacuate to its emergency fall-back location at Bangor in North Wales. There would be fewer places for research students than there had been in London. By then I had come to realize that I would never be an outstanding chemist. And I did not feel I should take up one of the scarce research places. Most importantly, I had to earn some money.

These were the last days of August 1939. All the news available pointed to the fact that Hitler would attack Poland. No one thought he would respond to the ultimatums of Britain and France. War seemed inevitable. And most people thought that there would be immediate air raids on London. My Spanish colleague Eduardo de Salas had likewise decided not to go to Bangor with the department; if war came he would have to go home to Spain. So we decided we would get out of London together, it didn't matter where, but somewhere towards the West. When we got to Paddington the station was in chaos. No one knew what trains were running and when. Thousands of people wanted to get out of London. So we got on a train at random and decided to get off at some small station. We got off at Wantage and walked through the little town into some farming country on its outskirts. There we asked at a farmhouse if we could have a room. Surprisingly – after all, foreigners were suspect when a war was about to break out – they offered us a room and told us we could have our meals with them.

We spent the next two or three days doing little else but listen to the news. At last, on 3 September, Neville Chamberlain announced that Hitler had failed to respond to the British and French ultimatum, and that Britain was therefore at war with Germany. The next day, or the day after, my landlady in London, to whom I had given my telephone number in Wantage, phoned to say there was a telegram for me. I asked her to read it to me: The BBC wanted me to report urgently to a particular room in Broadcasting House, at a given date at a given time. That sounded hopeful. I said goodbye to de Salas and returned to London. (Nearly sixty years later, when I found myself in Barcelona and saw his name in the telephone directory I phoned him and we had a brief reminiscing conversation.)

When I reported to the BBC, there were perhaps six or eight other people in the same room. An official, whom I later knew as John Kayser, informed us that a very secret department had been set up. He was not allowed to tell us anything about it: those of us who passed the test would be told what it was all about when we started work. For the moment, he would, in a few minutes, switch on the radio with the midday news from *Deutschlandsender*. We were to take down as much as we could. In the next room there were typewriters and we were to type out in English what we had heard in German. It so happened – one never knows in life what may come in useful – that I was a good German shorthand writer. In fact, some years earlier, I had come top out of all Prague German schools in a shorthand competition. I saw at once that I was getting a lot more down on paper than Mr Kayser, who seemed to be only jotting down cues. I typed out my translation and a few days later was informed that the BBC was offering me a job. I was to report to a particular ticket window at Paddington station, where I would be given a ticket to 'somewhere in the country'. The ticket clerk, evidently less security-conscious than the BBC, said in the hearing of the people in the queue behind me: 'Ah yes, somewhere in the country. That's Evesham.'

Wartime: Evesham

At Evesham I duly got off the train and there was a lady waiting for me with a car – Betty Buckle, the local billeting officer. My contract, incidentally, provided for an annual salary of £300 plus a free billet. I was taken to the house of what I discovered was a family of market gardeners, left my modest luggage there, and was driven out by Betty Buckle to Wood Norton, a Victorian Gothic country house a few miles outside Evesham, at one time the home of the Duc d'Orléans, the pretender to the French throne, whose fleur-de-lis was on every light switch. However, this splendid house was occupied by some section of the foreign-language service, I believe a South American one, while the Monitoring Service – I had by then been vouchsafed the name of the department by Betty Buckle – was established in a smaller building known as Mrs Smith's House. (Nobody seemed to know who Mrs Smith was.)

The first person I met was a man, younger than myself, wearing riding breeches. He introduced himself as Turli Weidenfeld. (Many years later he became Sir George Weidenfeld and later still, in Harold Wilson's retirement honours list, Lord Weidenfeld of Chelsea. He has been an enterprising and successful publisher, and I have translated about a dozen books for his firm. We are still friends.)

He took me to see 'the boss', Richard Marriott, who seemed only a few years older than myself and was the complete opposite of what the boss of an important government service would have been in Czechoslovakia. He received me sitting on top of his desk, dangling his feet, and told me a little about the work. This was then very secret and we all had to sign the Official Secrets Act. But by now a number of books have appeared about the service, so I can talk about it without risk of prosecution. There was a Listening Room with about ten positions. One listened-in with headphones, which were plugged into a selection switch: one was told on what line the station one was to listen in to would be found. (In later years monitors had their own specialized radio sets in front of them and had to tune in to their stations themselves.) Having listened to a broadcast, and taken as many notes as one could, one went to the Typing Room and dictated one's translation to a typist. Most of these girls had come from Television, which had been closed down on the outbreak of the war, and had been secretaries there; in other words, they were more highly educated than one would expect from merely a typist. One's 'transcript' next went to the Supervisors' Room, where it was sub-edited, or cut down, and then sent by teleprinter to London, to a News Bureau which then passed the material to the different ministries or intelligence agencies. (The structure and procedure, needless to say, underwent a great many changes in the light of experience in subsequent years.) As a back-up, and also for more detailed transcription, all the broadcasts fed to us on line were recorded on wax cylinders by a small team of engineers 'on top of the hill', where special aerials were located. They were brought down the hill to Mrs Smith's House in baskets by a small team of elderly men, oddly enough called 'boys' – apparently a tradition in newspaper offices. On rainy days the slopes of the hill were muddy and slippery and the wax cylinders quite often arrived broken, or at least cracked. It was impressed on us not to rely on them but to get down as much as possible while listening 'live'. This was often difficult, especially when reception was poor.

I was put, as a learner, under the guidance of a Mrs Gillespie, a formidable lady and strict tutor, but basically quite pleasant. I don't recall having had any problems with the monitoring of news bulletins or political talks – that was just the language of newspapers. However, our intelligence customers were interested just as much, and maybe even more, in German broadcasts for farmers – these, it was explained, might be informative on food shortages, crop expectations, and even the weather. (No country broadcast any weather forecasts during the war, for fear these might help enemy air raids.) Very early in my monitoring career I was assigned a farmers' talk about the servicing of cows by bulls. Bulls' semen was very valuable in wartime and none could be wasted. The broadcast explained in some detail how such wastage could be avoided. I was completely out of my depth. My English sexual vocabulary was based more on what one could read on lavatory walls than on scientific animal biology. But I had a wonderful typist. When I explained my predicament to her, she said: 'Don't worry. I am a farmer's daughter. You just use the words you know and I'll put it into the proper language.' And so she did. There was no embarrassment on either side – possibly because one felt that one was working for the war effort.

I must pay some tribute to the 'supervisors'. They included such people as the subsequently famous broadcaster Gilbert Harding, or Gustav Renier, the author of *The English, Are They Human?*, the charming Archie Gordon, who a few years later succeeded to the title of Marquess of Aberdeen and Temair, and quite a few well-known writers. It seems that, generally, literary people unsuitable, for some reason or other, for active military service, were directed by the authorities into the BBC or the Ministry of Information. Some of these supervisors, after butchering our generally poor English, would seek us out afterwards and with great kindness explain where we offended against grammar or syntax or style. I have said so before – but my overwhelming impression of the English during my early years in England, whether at the university or at the BBC, was the courteous way they treated me as an equal. No one, then or later, ever 'pulled rank' with me; no one ever exhibited any xenophobia. A class-ridden society England may have been – but I never felt it on my skin.

On the other hand, my faith in the patriotism of the British was shaken by my billetors. They were farmers or market gardeners. At breakfast, which, my shifts permitting, I had with them, I repeatedly heard them making what to me seemed unpatriotic remarks. Whenever the Minister of Food imposed some new regulation or restriction, they would refuse to carry it out and decided instead to grow luxury crops, like asparagus, for the hotel and restaurant trade. When there was some talk about destroying crops in the event of a German invasion, they declared that they wouldn't dream of doing that – after all, the Germans would want to eat too, wouldn't they?

The first winter of the war was exceptionally cold. My room, of course, was unheated and every morning I had to knock the ice out of my frozen shaving brush. Some time during the winter I developed a serious cold, with a temperature. And I remember Richard Marriott, the head of the service, coming to visit me – how many bosses in Prague would have visited a sick underling? – and telling my landlady that an unheated room was not the right place for a sick person. I think I was then provided with an electric fire.

We worked three shifts, from 8 am to 4 pm, from 4 pm to midnight, and from midnight to 8 am. Although there were no German home service broadcasts after midnight, the German external service, from Zeesen, beamed mainly to America, had to be covered. During the day two German stations – *Deutschlandsender* and Hamburg were continuously 'watched' in case there were special announcements at unscheduled times. Watch duty was shared fairly among monitors and was popular because one could read a book or the paper while listening to (mostly) good music. The BBC provided a bus service between Evesham and Wood Norton, but most of us had bicycles and, at least in good weather, preferred to be independent. I even remember walking back from Wood Norton to Evesham for exercise – it was probably not much more than two miles. One of our more eccentric colleagues, Jacques Nield, on at least one occasion turned up on horseback, along with another colleague, Doreen Urwick. I think they just tethered their horses to the ornamental gate, known as the Golden Gate. Jacques was not only eccentric but also irascible: I more than once watched him pick up a typewriter – these were heavy old-fashioned machines – and angrily fling it to the floor. But he was a good linguist – also, as a hobby, an Egyptologist who could read hieroglyphs – and, irascible or not, he stayed with the service until he died. I recall another eccentric incident from the early days of the war. A dashing young Polish monitor, whose name I have forgotten, one day turned up for late shift wearing tails and white tie: he was going on to some formal party.

Considering that there was a war on and that Evesham was a small provincial town we had quite a busy social life. The reason, of course, was that we had no 'home'. Our billets were just for sleeping. But there was a BBC Club, a good-sized building on Green Hill with spacious rooms, a small room with a table-tennis table and, most importantly for many of us who did not get these facilities in our billets, a modern bathroom (which, admittedly, one had to book in advance). In the evenings there was gramophone music and dancing.

Evesham is on the River Avon, and I remember some very enjoyable picnics on a grassy spot that was reached only by rowing there. I even think one had to pull one's boat up over the rollers by the weir. Many of us had bikes and we would ride, in groups of up to ten or twelve, to the many pubs in the neighbourhood. Broadway was only a few miles away and we discovered that – perhaps an oversight by those making the regulations – there was a shop there that made and sold fudge at a time when chocolate was severely rationed. I also remember playing tennis in Evesham, but only once or twice. But I played a lot of table tennis at the Club.

There were also regular dances at the Crown Hotel, of Evesham's allegedly exclusive 'Twenty Club', to which I went frequently, always with the same partner, Audrey Brayshaw, one of our typists and a very pretty girl. It was a totally chaste and purely friendly partnership just for those dances. Some of us also had a favourite teashop at the very centre of the town, the Gateway Café, where we were often entertained by Weidenfeld's brilliant – but of course invented – dialogues between Hitler and Mussolini, through Hitler's interpreter Herr Schmidt. Weidenfeld had a great talent for impersonation: his Hitler and Mussolini sounded absolutely authentic. Schmidt I had never heard, no one probably had, but the way Weidenfeld, whose Italian was fluent, made him translate the two dictators' words was extremely funny.

Mary, who had graduated just before the war, was then working as a chemist for the Northern Aluminium Company in Banbury – not too far away. So when a Polish colleague was selling his car for £20 I jumped at the opportunity. It was a Hillman Minx in good condition, and the reason he was selling it was that petrol was rationed and he had little use for it. But it struck me that it was just the thing to get me to Banbury or to some halfway point between us. I had taken a driving test in Prague almost as soon as I was old enough, but I had to get an English driving licence. I failed at the first attempt but succeeded at the second. In the end I didn't use the car for that purpose, but instead saved up my petrol coupons. It was perfectly easy to get to Banbury by train, which I did a few times to go to dances there. We also sometimes met at Stratford and went to the Playhouse.

Soon my domestic arrangements in Evesham were to improve dramatically. A Russian colleague of mine, Shurrah (Alexander) Elkin – actually a supervisor, not a monitor – who had an Irish wife and did not fancy staying in a billet, decided to buy a house and asked me if I would like to share it with them. I would, technically, be their lodger: I would have my own room, but I would of course be free to share their sitting room, kitchen, etc. I jumped at the offer. They were a very nice couple and I was by then rather tired of my market-garden landlords. The Elkins' house was on Port Street, only a few steps from the final stop of the BBC bus.

By then the monitoring staff had grown and there were some interesting and brilliant people on it. The one to become most famous after the war was Ernst (later Sir Ernst) Gombrich, later still awarded the exclusive Order of Merit. Gombrich came from Vienna, from a family of musicians, and had studied history of art. He came to England after the Warburg Institute transferred from Germany and worked there as a research scholar. After his war work at the BBC he returned to the Warburg Institute, by then as its Director. His wife Ilse came from Czechoslovakia – she speaks both English and German with a Czech accent to this day. Gombrich and I got on very well together and we sometimes, when we were both on night shift and nothing much was happening, competed with each other translating Petrarch's sonnets. In recent years I had been visiting him at his home in north London about once a year. Sadly, when I telephoned him before our departure for Florida in November 2001, his son – himself a distinguished scholar – answered the phone and told me that his father had died the day before.

Another art historian was Ernst Buschbeck, also from Vienna. Before the Anschluss he had been the director of the Kunsthistorisches Museum and he resumed this post immediately after the war. A monarchist at heart, a cavalry captain in the First World War, he was the embodiment of Vienna under the Habsburg monarchy. But he had a very lively mind and was knowledgeable in all kinds of directions. He died tragically in Cornwall, several years after the war, when a freak wave snatched him from a rock and he was drowned. Another outstanding figure was Anatole Goldberg, a superb linguist, equally fluent in Russian, German and English. After some time in Evesham he was 'poached' by the External Service and soon became the star commentator of its Russian section. He became enormously popular in the Soviet Union, where the BBC in Russian was widely listened to: people believed it, whereas they did not believe their own broadcasts. His political commentaries went out in Russian and in English. He had an uncanny knack of 'writing to time'. If told that his contribution had to be seventeen minutes, he would sit down and write it, and would never be more than a few seconds out. His broadcasts never had to be cut or 'padded'. And alongside his work in the BBC he managed to write a successful biography of Ilya Ehrenburg. And finally there was Martin Esslin, originally Pereszlenyi, who later became a well-known theatre scholar with famous books about Bertold Brecht and about the Theatre of the Absurd. At one time he held a professorship at Stanford University near San Francisco, became Head of BBC Drama and received an OBE from The Queen.

It is really quite remarkable how the BBC built up a reputation for truthfulness and reliability – not only during the war, but long after the war. The Nazis confiscated and prohibited short-wave radios not because they were afraid of the effect of British 'propaganda' broadcasts, but of the effect of straight news bulletins. It is a humbling thought that people in occupied Europe, and later in the Soviet sphere of Europe, risked imprisonment and sometimes death, in order to find out what was really happening in the world. I spoke to many people after the war, in Germany and in Czechoslovakia, and was invariably told that far more people listened to the BBC than to the lavishly endowed American-sponsored stations like The Voice of America and Radio Free Europe. While I think that this reputation was justified, and while I am proud that, in a very small measure, my work may have contributed to it, honesty nevertheless compels me, in what, after all, is a kind of historical record, to admit that the truthfulness of BBC news bulletins was not quite a hundred percent. We were far more frank with our home audiences and with our audiences abroad than any other government in wartime – but not completely. I was one of the people allowed to see a highly confidential daily intelligence report, the 'Newsome report', and distinctly remember that, at the height of the U-boat battle, we did not always admit the full extent of our losses. We lost so-and-so-many ships, the report stated, but we are admitting only to so-and-so-many. Psychological warfare historians may say that this was done to keep the enemy guessing, rather than to deceive the home public. There may be some truth in that, but it qualifies to some degree the 'absolute truthfulness' claim of the BBC. Exaggerated figures of enemy aircraft shot down during the Battle of Britain, on the other hand, were probably not due to deliberate deception, but rather to the fact that more than one RAF fighter pilot – in good faith – claimed the destruction of the same German machine. These figures were also subsequently revised. Yes, on balance, we are entitled to be proud to have been as truthful as we were.

Most people will have forgotten that during the first winter of the war virtually nothing happened at the fronts and, indeed, very little in the air. This was what the British called the 'phoney war' and the French *drôle de guerre.* No particular activity was therefore expected over Christmas, especially as the German broadcasts took on a very maudlin and sentimental tone. It was therefore decided that the German 'watch' and 'coverage' could be safely left in the hands of two, by then reasonably experienced, monitors – Otto Giles and myself. Otto was some years older than me, had studied law at Breslau (now Wróclaw in Poland) and was a qualified English lawyer. In the entrance hall of Mrs Smith's House, which was not suitable, or at least not used, for any operational purposes, our thoughtful boss, Richard Marriott, had arranged for a table-tennis table to be set up, and monitors in-between duty used it quite a lot. (There was nothing else to do since Wood Norton was too far out of Evesham.) To Otto's and my great delight Marriott, a few days before Christmas, appeared with two pairs of headphones on lines about 10 metres long, to enable us, while on the 'Christmas watch', to play table-tennis downstairs while being plugged in to Hamburg and *Deutschlandsender* upstairs. If anything happened outside the scheduled bulletin times we would just rush upstairs and do our job. Nothing of the kind happened and I have recollections of prolonged table tennis games. To the Czech reader this may seem almost a *Švejkovština*, but it was nothing of the kind. The British took the war very seriously, but sport to them was likewise a serious business. And it showed that a highly disciplined service could be run in a very human way, without Prussian drill.

An amusing sidelight on the BBC's mores at the time concerns female staff on night shift. One has to remember the prewar history of the BBC under the directorship of Lord Reith, a man of great rectitude but also some Scottish primness. In his day news readers – remember: on the radio, not on television – had to wear dinner jackets for reading the evening news. A gentleman simply wore evening dress after certain hours, whether he was seen by anyone else or not. And female staff were never allowed to work at night.

Like a lot of other practices, these had obviously to be discontinued in wartime. It was clear that operational necessity required typists to work night shifts – but the management continued to be a little uneasy about this. The girls, not unreasonably, wanted to wear trousers. And, if you come think about it, this was probably a lot more 'moral' than wearing skirts. But a lady simply did not (then) wear trousers, except perhaps for riding or skiing. After some negotiation with her superiors, the Monitoring Service personnel officer – who I think sided with the girls – eventually issued an edict to the effect that female staff on shifts after a certain hour (I think: probably after 'office hours') could wear trousers, provided these were of 'subdued' or 'dark' colour – black, navy, or dark green. I don't really think that any of our typists would have wanted to wear white, cream or pink trousers, but I remember that the ruling, when posted on the notice board, caused a good deal of amusement.

More and more huts were being built in the grounds of Wood Norton, camouflaged and hidden under the trees. One, a fairly large one, had been there when I arrived: this was the canteen. Perhaps one's expectations were not very high in wartime, with most foodstuffs being rationed, but I remember the canteen food to have been rather good.

Whereas during the first few months of my work I had been a German monitor exclusively, I later also became a part-time Czech monitor. The news from the Protectorate service in Prague was of no interest: it was simply a translation of the German news bulletins. But there were occasional propaganda talks that were worth transcribing. On one occasion I remember monitoring an almost inaudible Czech broadcast from a transmitter in New York. And when a Free Czechoslovak Army was set up in France it was given Fécamp radio for its own broadcasts. We covered that too.

Some time during the summer of 1940 monitoring operations moved from Mrs Smith's house to the new huts. The primitive arrangement of recordings being made on top of the hill was discontinued: now the recording machines, still working with wax cylinders, were located in the Listening Room, at each listening position, and we operated them ourselves. This saved a lot of time and cut out the risk of damage to the cylinders on the slippery way down from the hill.

At about that time the Monitoring Service was made a 'defence establishment'. A tall wire fence was erected all around the Wood Norton grounds and a unit of regular soldiers was stationed there to protect it. We were rather scared of them: they seemed a very simple-minded, not to say stupid, lot who weren't quite sure what to make of a place where so many foreigners worked. The sentries at the gate through the wire did not just check our identity cards, but invariably went through the whole traditional drill, which probably dated from the Napoleonic wars. As soon as they spotted you approaching, they would shout: 'Halt! Who goes there?' At which – this had been hammered into us – you had to stop ('freeze', as they say in American movies) and shout back: 'Friend!' To which the sentry would reply: 'Advance, friend, and be recognized.' Only then, with the sentry's rifle still pointed at your chest, did you approach and present your identity pass. After dark this could be quite unnerving.

All of us also had to undergo fire drill. (This seemed a lot more sensible.) A person – and I think this applied only to the male staff – was trained either as a Number One, or a Number Two, or a Number Three. The Number One was the person holding the nozzle of the hose, nearest the fire. The Number Two was responsible for looking after the hose –

moving it, ensuring that it was not twisted or had kinks in it. The Number Three was the man at the hydrant, or at the pump, and was responsible for the supply of water. Needless to say, I was a Number Three.

When, shortly afterwards, a real fire broke out in the 'great house' I was not on duty, and by the time I heard about it the fire had been put out – not by our fire-fighting team but by the regular fire brigade. They did not rely on the local water supply, but ran long hoses down into the river. Apparently the authorities ordered a fighter plane to patrol over the property in case the glow of the fire attracted enemy aircraft. Damage was considerable: the top floor of the great house was gutted. All the men were also given a course in 'Unarmed combat'. This involved, among other things, disarming a person attacking you with a hand-held bayonet and abseiling from an upstairs window of Mrs Smith's house. I still cannot envisage any military situation that might have called for these skills from us.

At one point somebody in authority decided that we should get a monitor who could handle the Berber language, though there was only one station in North Africa which – and that only occasionally – broadcast in it. Maybe the memory of Lawrence of Arabia organizing the 'Revolt in the Desert' against the Turks played a part in this decision. So one day a swarthy young man appeared, in a gaudy uniform that would have been a little outré even for a British general. As he didn't speak a word of English he was accompanied by a young North African Jew as his permanent interpreter. The Berber had to be dismissed within a few days: he just couldn't see a girl without trying to rape her on the spot.

The occupation of Belgium and the Netherlands, the fall of France and the rescue of the mauled British Expeditionary Force from Dunkirk did not in themselves affect the smooth professional operation of the Monitoring Service, except that there were now a lot more Nazi radio stations that had to be listened to – not only in German, but also in French and Dutch.

Some time after the establishment of a Czechoslovak Army in Britain, and of other exile armies, the British parliament passed the Allied Forces War Service Act. This extended the liability for military service, which already existed for British subjects, to the nationals of Britain's allies. The Act, however, gave such nationals an option: if, for whatever reason, they did not wish to serve in their own government's armed forces, they could opt for service in the British forces. Work in the Monitoring Service was a 'reserved occupation'. However, when the

Allied Forces War Service Act came into force, those of us who were allied nationals asked our superiors what to do – as indeed we were required under our service contract. Our superiors got in touch with the British authorities (the Ministry of Labour and National Service) and also with the Czechoslovak foreign ministry in London. Both were anxious to keep us in the Monitoring Service. But in order to comply with the requirements of the Allied Forces War Service Act they came up with the ingenious (or perhaps devious) solution that we should volunteer for active service, but choose the 'British option'; the British authorities would then exempt us from active service. This is what we did and what happened. Everyone was happy except the Czechoslovak military authorities (who had always regarded the 'British option' as incompatible with Czechoslovak law). After the conclusion of the war it became clear that I, and some of my colleagues, had become victims of an inter-departmental conflict within the Czechoslovak exile authorities. While the political branch, the foreign ministry and its embassy in London gave me a certificate to the effect that I had behaved as a 'loyal citizen' and happily renewed my Czechoslovak passport, the military branch declared that I was not a citizen because I had not fulfilled my military obligations. I should have volunteered for the Czechoslovak army before the Allied Forces legislation was passed. None of this worried me at the time, especially as my naturalization as a British subject came through very soon, out of turn, in recognition of my war work. But some fifty years later, in connection with a restitution claim, this proved a real obstacle.

In the early summer of 1941 Hitler invaded the Soviet Union. Almost overnight, the Soviet Union, until then an ally of Germany and the occupying power of half of Poland, became an ally of the Western Powers. The Monitoring Service responded by increasing the number of its Russian monitors. One wall of the 'News Bureau' – the part of the service directly in touch with government quarters – was covered with a huge map, or a number of maps joined together, on which the German-Soviet frontline was shown with a thread of red wool, repositioned every day in the light of monitored material. I remember a group of two or three high-ranking Soviet officers, from the Soviet military mission in London, coming down to Evesham and studying this map with enormous interest. The official information they were getting from the USSR, they frankly admitted, was not to be trusted.

There was another amusing occasion involving a Soviet general. One of our Russian supervisors was André Belosselsky – his full name being His Serene Highness Prince André Sergeevich Belosselsky-Belozersky, though he never made anything of the fact that he came from the highest rank of the Russian nobility. His father, the 'old prince', then about fifty, had been the hereditary cup-bearer to the Russian tsar. One of our Russian monitors, Nina Burch, gave a Russian party at her house and – rather naughtily, some of us thought – invited a general from the Soviet mission in London as well as the old Prince Belosselsky. Yet the meeting, according to witnesses, went very well: the prince – who had been forced to escape from Russia after the Bolshevik takeover in 1917 – drew himself up and introduced himself: 'Prince Sergey Sergeevich Belosselsky-Belozersky, hereditary cup-bearer to His Imperial Majesty'. The Soviet general likewise clicked his heels and introduced himself, the two men saluted, shook hands, and apparently got on splendidly, discussing military operations. (That was not until after the service had moved from Evesham to Caversham Park near Reading.)

Sharing a house with Shurrah and Muriel Elkin was to have important consequences for my later life. Shurrah's elderly parents were living in London. Thus, when the German air raids began, Shurrah rented the house next door, which happened to be vacant, and brought his parents down to Evesham. Boris Isakovich and Anna Alexandrovna were a charming couple, educated Russian intellectuals, liberals who had supported the 1905 democratic revolution, but had emigrated to Berlin after the 1917 Bolshevik revolution. I am not sure when they came to England, but I think it must have been in the early 1930s. After a few weeks in Evesham they got rather bored and one day asked me if I would allow them to teach me Russian. Of course I gladly accepted their offer. It was mostly Anna Alexandrovna who taught me, and she was a good teacher.

A little while into my 'Russian studies' it occurred to me that, especially since I had no academic degree, I might as well legitimize my studies by entering the University of London as an 'external student' of 'Russian Language and Literature' with (because I thought this would be easy) German as my 'secondary subject'. The Russian course was far from easy: it included quite a lot of Old Church Slavonic, fortunately not too much Old Russian, a 'general' literature paper, and a 'special period' (for which I chose 1800-1848, the Russian classical period). Although the degree course – a so-called 'honours course' – was just as tough as in peacetime, the university was very considerate in terms of exam schedules for 'students engaged in war work'. One was (more or less) free to choose when to sit one's exam. Languages had always been a particular interest of mine and, more importantly, I felt that studying for a degree might not only be useful for after the war, but even during the war would be a good counterweight to the largely passive work of listening to enemy broadcasts. And, once more, I was lucky. One of my colleagues, Herbert Goldstaub (but later Professor Herbert Galton of the University of Kansas), had taken Slavonic studies in Vienna under the famous Professor Count Trubetzkoy and still had all his lecture notes. He generously lent me these, and I got down to work. I had to order a lot of books from libraries, and buy quite a lot myself, especially textbooks of Old Church Slavonic, and textbooks of Russian literature. Alongside these more theoretical studies I was being taught Russian by old Mrs Elkin, and before long I read *War and Peace* in the original, as well as a lot of Lermontov and Pushkin. My choice of German as my 'secondary subject' proved a lot more difficult than I had expected – a much more thorough knowledge of Middle High German (grammar and literature) was called for than I had done at school in Prague. To cut a long story short, I sat my exams at intervals throughout the war, but did not actually sit my Finals until 1949. I got an Upper Second – I had hoped for a First, but I discovered that no external student had ever got a First in Russian.

It must have been in the early 1940s that I took up again my idea of producing an anthology of Czech poetry in English translation. Having failed, before the war, to interest any of the leading English poets in the idea, I now found a colleague who embraced the idea with enthusiasm. J.K. Montgomery was one of the oldest of my colleagues: he had lived in Italy and was employed as an Italian monitor, but he had published a volume of his own poetry and had a genuine skill for translating rhymed verse. The principal difficulty, I remember, was getting our material together. No British library then had Czech poetry, no British university had a Czech department. But I wrote to friends and acquaintances, and eventually managed to get a reasonably representative, if small, collection of 20th century Czech poetry together – starting about the turn of the century, with Březina and Machar, and going as 'up to date' as some Nezval, Hora and Seifert poems written during the war and published in London under the auspices of Beneš's exile government. We worked quite hard at the project: I would make a word-for-word translation, setting out the rhythm and the rhyme scheme, explaining allusions, etc., and my colleague would turn these into English poems.

To anticipate: this volume, *Modern Czech Poetry*, was eventually published in 1945, just about the time the war ended. I have in my archive – now kept at the Památník národního písemnictví in Prague – the copy of a letter from Jan Masaryk, then the Czechoslovak foreign minister, to the British Controller of Paper Supplies (paper was still strictly rationed at the time), requesting him to release enough paper for a small print run of this volume. This was the first of my published translations in book form; individual translations of poems had already appeared in the *Central European Observer*, a weekly published by the Czechoslovak exile government, and in an Anglo-Czechoslovak cultural periodical, *Review-41 to 47* – its editors were Pavel Tigrid, Karel Brušák and Valter Berger – to which I frequently contributed during the war, also with a lot of unsigned translations, and the London editorship of which I took over shortly after the war, when the three editors returned to Prague. I was very proud of my first published book, and although nowadays – about 150 books later – each new publication gives me a lot of pleasure, that thrill of my first book was something different.

A few of these translations were of poems by Vítězslav Nezval, from his surrealist volume *Prague with Rain Fingers*. These appealed to me greatly, but not to my collaborator Montgomery – so I translated these on my own. Some time towards the end of the war they appeared in *Daylight and New Writing*, published by John Lehmann. Other translations from *Modern Czech Poetry* were included, actually without my knowledge, my consent being taken for granted, in two major anthologies of Czechoslovak writing published during the late stages of the war in America: *Hundred Towers* and *Heart of Europe* – my first 'publications' in the United States

By the time I joined the Monitoring Service in the autumn of 1939 I had translated and published perhaps two dozen Czech and Lachian poems, and published about half a dozen of my own poems written in German. But it was my work in the BBC Monitoring Service that turned me into a professional translator. The demand for accuracy – the Prime Minister and the government might base their decisions on your information – and the time pressure (the longer a translation took the more it lost in importance) provided a relentless schooling. Ernst Gombrich has said that the Monitoring Service had taught him English. I would say that no doubt it improved my English and that it certainly taught me to translate.

In later life, as a literary translator, I always declared that I only translated poetry and prose that spoke to me, that turned me on, and that I never embarked on a translation that left me cold or (worse) disgusted me. As a monitor I could not indulge in such luxury. I frequently had to translate speeches and articles that I found outrageous and sickening – such as Hitler's speeches or Goebbels's articles in *Das Reich*. One simply had to achieve some detachment from these texts, one had to forget, while translating them, that one was one of the `subhumans' that the Nazi leaders were ranting against and whom they hoped to exterminate. Surprisingly, in retrospect, this detachment was not difficult to achieve.

It may well be that my on-duty translating of enemy broadcasts had something to do with the fact that in my later `off-duty' translation work I invariably only dealt with material that attracted me.

I am sometimes asked if I like translating poetry better than translating prose. I have no general answer to this question. And although I have always chosen the poetry I wanted to translate, I have quite often – e.g. with Thomas Bernhard or Ivan Klíma – greatly enjoyed translating the prose books offered me by publishers.

Work in the Monitoring Service continued to be exciting, and also exhausting. And at the back of my mind was my constant worry about my mother and my brother.

Meanwhile Mary was working in London as a chemist for a pharmaceutical firm, staying at the YWCA, which happened to be quite close to her laboratory. I usually came up to London over the weekend, staying at a cheap hotel just across the road from the YWCA. In retrospect we are both surprised at our total lack of fear at the time, even though this was the peak period of the German air raids on London. In some strange way we felt we were immune, untouchable. We would go out to restaurants to dine, and we would sit until late at night in the basement café of a Lyons Corner House. And we would go to the cinema. I distinctly remember seeing Charlie Chaplin in *The Great Dictator*, that brilliant film making fun of Hitler, with German bombs dropping close enough for the whole cinema to shake. On another occasion, the weekend of the famous 'Bloomsbury raid', I woke up at night in my hotel after what sounded like a very close bomb burst. I opened my room door and noticed with a sense of shock, that all the shoes – in those days hotels still cleaned your shoes overnight – had disappeared except mine. I quickly dressed, put on my shoes, and walked downstairs. I found all the hotel staff and the guests crowded in the hotel's boiler room. (Jiří Mucha much later wrote up this story.) They were amazed to see me walk in: they had assumed that everyone had heard the hotel alarm and come down at the time. After the All Clear – it was still dark – I went out into the street. Buildings all round, quite close, were wrecked or in flames. Fortunately the YWCA, just as my hotel, had escaped unscathed. In the early morning Mary and I walked along Gower Street, ankle deep in rubble and broken glass. Our old college, University College in Gower Street, had received a direct hit and its cupola had gone. Rescue teams were already at work. This was probably the closest that we ever came to being killed by German bombs.

In the summer of 1941 – Mary and I were by then engaged – we decided to drive to the Lake District, which Mary knew from previous visits. We had saved up enough petrol coupons and we had a touching confidence in the performance of our little prewar car. Actually, the trip did not go too badly: apart from, at times, being very unwilling to start, and at others suddenly dying without any obvious cause, the engine behaved reasonably well. The thing was one could not risk stopping unless one had to – I remember we developed a technique for asking our way just by slowing down, without coming to a stop, and making the person we asked for information trot alongside our vehicle. But it was a wonderful holiday, with a lot of fell walking.

In 1942 we got married: it was a fairly simple wartime wedding, in Marlow, Mary's birthplace, with a reception in her parents' garden. The weather was perfect, her father's roses were in full bloom. We had a week's honeymoon in Scotland, at a small hotel at Bridge of Orchy, in Argyllshire, a little north of Loch Lomond, and near Glencoe. We had a lot of trout, freshly caught for us to order, and we walked quite a bit. The weather was perfect.

Caversham Park

Most historians agree in regarding 1942 as the turning point in the war – this was the year of Rommel's defeat in the Battle of El Alamein in North Africa and of the annihilation of the German Sixth Army at Stalingrad. In consequence, the authorities who decided the fate of our Monitoring Service concluded that the time had come to move it closer to London. Evesham had originally been chosen because it would be safe from German bombs – actually two or three bombs dropped on Evesham, though luckily into the river. But these were not deliberate: they were dropped by German bombers anxious to get rid of their bomb load on their way back home from raiding Birmingham. From the operational point of view Evesham was too far from London for efficient contact: not everything could be sent by teleprinter, there were bulky packages of monitored material that were conveyed by train every day, in the care of the guard, and collected by a government messenger when the train arrived at Paddington station. Now it was decided to move the service to Caversham Park, near Reading, only half an hour by train from London. Caversham Park was a big country house built in the nineteenth century, standing in a large park, and had, until early 1943, been used by the Oratory School, a Catholic public school. The first BBC personnel to move in were the engineers who installed not only dozens of miles of cables inside the building, but also a number of land lines to a nearby secluded property, Crowsley Park, where big aerials were rigged up for the reception of the more difficult signals.

The move itself was a masterpiece of planning and organization: it was performed in two days without any interruption or even reduction of the service. About half the staff were moved on Day 1 and immediately started monitoring a schedule worked out in detail, while the other half, still working at Wood Norton, were moved to Caversham Park on Day 2. It was a seamless operation.

The billeting system by then no longer applied. Our salaries had gone up, but we had to find, and pay for, our accommodation ourselves. Our own problem was that Mary was still working in London as a chemist and that we therefore needed to live within reasonable distance from a railway station. Our first room was with a pleasant couple, but the arrangement involved meals provided by them, and we really wanted to be independent. So we found another place, this time in Shiplake, quite near the railway station. But it was far from ideal. Almost as soon as we moved in, the owner, a Mrs Clark, whose husband was in the forces, asked me to drown a rat she had caught in a trap. (There was a stream, the Lashbrook, at the bottom of the garden.) Next, after offering to dry our bedding – our new bedlinen provided by Mary's mother, a kind of trousseau – Mrs Clark confessed that she had accidentally burnt it by trying to air it in her oven. And some time later – this was not Mrs Clark's fault – the ceiling fell down on us as we were in bed, due, apparently, to our own aircraft circling low overhead, getting into formation for a raid. We were covered in jagged pieces of plaster and in white dust, but luckily quite unscathed. Incidentally, I had to cycle to work from there, probably something like 40 minutes.

About that time all young male staff were encouraged to join the newly established Home Guard. After the fall of France a German invasion of England was a very real possibility, and today of course we know that *Unternehmen Seelöwe* [Operation Sea Lion] had been seriously planned by Hitler and had only been abandoned when the German Navy informed him that it could not guarantee the safety of the troops in the face of the British air force. The Home Guard was not, or not everywhere, the joke force portrayed in the TV serial *Dad's Army*. Indeed on one occasion our Home Guard battalion, in a night exercise against a regular Army battalion, won the exercise and captured the 'enemy' headquarters. I can claim no part in this achievement: I spent the whole night lying in a cold and damp hollow in the ground, and the only 'action' I saw was the umpires passing me twice. Our rifle firing and hand-grenade training was quite efficient, and I think we would have made quite a good job of guarding power stations, railway crossings, and so on. But there was an awful lot of ridiculous parade-ground drill, including such stuff as 'saluting to the right', 'saluting to the left', saluting a flag or a war memorial on the march, and so on. Hardly the stuff with which to oppose an invading modern army. I rose to the dizzy rank of corporal – which is what Napoleon and Hitler started out from. I was a good shot with a rifle and twice represented our platoon at national competitions at Bisley. Needless to say, without ever winning any trophy. But I was a very poor shot with a pistol or submachine-gun. And because I had once been a chemical student I was made the battalion's 'gas officer' and attended a number of lectures and gas exercises.

It must have been during the later stages of the war, probably in 1944, that, in connection with the occasional translations I did for the Czechoslovak government-in-exile I met Jiří Mucha, who was working at the government building, the Fursecroft in George Street, as a liaison officer between the Czechoslovak army and the government. Right from our first meeting we got on well together. The first thing of his that he asked me to translate was a poem about an air raid – not bad, but not outstandingly good. I think he was really a prose writer, and what is more, an excellent prose writer. Soon he gave me, at intervals, some short stories in an army setting which, he said, John Lehmann was interested in for his newly started series *Penguin New Writing*. I liked those stories, translated them, and very soon they appeared in *Penguin New Writing*. Before long John Lehmann – who had meanwhile taken over control of The Hogarth Press, the publishing house started by Virginia and Leonard Woolf – decided to collect these stories and bring them out in book form under the title *The Problems of Lieutenant Knap*. This appeared in 1945, very shortly after the end of the war, and was my first volume of prose translations.

Under the terms of my BBC contract, because of the then secrecy of the monitoring operation, I had to obtain written permission for anything that was published by me, whether under my name or anonymously – even quite brief book reviews. But the BBC was an enlightened employer and permission was invariably given.

During the war I also met Viktor Fischl, who was then working for the Czechoslovak government in London. I remember translating one of his stories, *The Trap* [*Past*], but I do not think it was ever published. He now lives in Israel under the name of Avigdor Dagan, but comes to Prague every year.

I also had a lot of contact, during and immediately after the war, with Eduard Goldstücker, who was then in the diplomatic service. We often had lunch together in the Czechoslovak Restaurant in Edgware Road, discussing political and literary topics. On one occasion – Mary and I were living in London by then – I was giving him a lift in our ancient little car to Buckingham Palace, where he was to present his credentials, and we had a skid in the middle of Piccadilly. A 180-degree skid, ending up neatly facing the opposite way on the opposite side of the road – a stunt driver could not have done it better if he had tried. So we calmly did a U turn and I delivered him safely to just outside the Palace. I cannot remember why he should have needed me. The last time I saw him, rather shrunk but as bright and alert as ever, was when, himself in his middle eighties, he introduced a little Festschrift produced for me by the Jednota tlumočníků a překladatelů, the Czech Union of Interpreters and Translators, entitled *Kosmdesátinám Ewalda Oserse* [*On Ewald Osers's Eightieth Birthday*]. I had not been told in advance that he would be doing that and I was very touched. Sadly he died in 2001.

Soon after the end of the war one of the editors of *Review-41* – which by then had become *Review-45* – Valter Berger, decided to return to Prague and handed over to us the unexpired lease of his flat in London. This was in a fortress-like block of flats (illustrated in some histories of modern architecture) in Shepherds Bush Road in West London, called The Grampians. It was a small flat on the first floor – small hall, living room, bedroom, kitchen and bathroom – but we were glad to get it. It was the first place of our own. In the hall there was a cupboard door into a waste-disposal chute – then a very modern facility, except that on one occasion a burglar got into our flat that way while we were out. He must have been disturbed, because all he got away with was our ration books.

Our roles were now reversed: it was I who did the commuting to work, whereas Mary could get to work by Underground. Commuting was not too bad. A BBC car would take me to Reading station, from where I took a train to Paddington, from where I got to Shepherds Bush by tube. I had a season ticket, and when I was on a late shift the railway staff very obligingly allowed me to get on one of their many 'ghost trains' that ran during the night for the benefit of railway staff. Quite often these stopped at Westbourne Park, which was more convenient for me than going all the way to Paddington. I certainly don't remember it as a hardship.

One condition that went with the flat was that I would take on the 'London office' of *Review-45*. This was not too much work, and I quite enjoyed it. My duties included choosing submitted articles, stories and poems for publication, and sometimes even soliciting contributions. My proudest achievement was when I persuaded T.S. Eliot to send us an article for publication, and my least proud achievement was rejecting (several times) stories by Wolf Mankowitz, who later became a very well-known and frequently published author. (I console myself with the thought that the French translation of *Gone with the Wind* had been rejected by seventeen publishers before one publisher finally accepted it. Editorial decisions are not an exact science.)

About the end of the war I received news of my family. A cousin-once-removed, Kirk (formerly Kurt) Petshek (formerly Petschek), was serving in the US forces, in the Strategic Bombing Survey, and with his unit had gone to (by then) occupied Germany and, on an unofficial mission, had gone to Prague. He sent back word that my brother had survived, but that my mother had perished in the Holocaust. I will not go here into the exciting story of my brother's escape from Zamość in Poland – he is one of only five known survivors. His story has been published and repeatedly broadcast by Prague radio. Just before the end of the war my brother, by then in Slovakia, had, through an amazing coincidence, received news that I was alive. The Beneš government, with some of its staff, had by then returned to the liberated part of Czechoslovakia, and there, in the streets of Košice, my brother encountered a classmate, Hana Stránská, who had then been working for a number of years for the Czechoslovak government-in-exile. Only the previous week, she told him, she had spoken to me in London.

We stayed in London for a little over a year. London then was very different from what it has become today. One reason, of course, was that petrol was still in very short supply; another was that numerous businesses that had been bombed out of London and had set up offices out of town had not yet returned. The whole City and the East End were devastated – the degree of the destruction was much more extensive than the media had suggested during the war. Somehow I had got our ancient little car to London and kept it at a workshop and filling station in Chiswick, not too far from our flat. But I don't think I used it a lot. Indeed, after our adventurous drive to the Lake District the year before we were married, we used the train for our holidays, though we always took our bicycles with us. I distinctly remember that we were in the Lake District again, in a small place called Seathwaite, when we listened on the radio to the news of the liberation of Paris. We also went to Wales with our bikes and did a great deal of cycling there.

While we were living in London we also quite often went to the theatre, to concerts and to the opera. About that time I also – I no longer remember how – came to know Fred Marnau. He was a Jewish refugee from Bratislava, a man with literary interests and, in some ways, a protégé of Stephen Spender's. He wrote a very fine cycle of poems entitled *The Wounds of the Apostles*. I used to visit him quite often at his office at the top of Kingsway. Not until many years later, and then by pure accident, did I discover that those pre-war cultural supplements to *Prager Presse* that contained my German translations of Czech poetry also contained some of his German translations of Slovak poets. He is no longer alive.

The final phase of the war, needless to say, brought a great deal of excitement. The Prague Rising in May 1945 was covered entirely by a Czech colleague, George Langweil, and myself. The transmitter the Czech resistance fighters had taken over, Praha II, was a weak local transmitter and even with our special aerials reception was very faint. I shall never forget the terrible twenty minutes or so, when the radio desperately called for help against German tanks moving towards Prague on the something-or-other road. Langweil and I tried every listening trick we knew to make out the words by replaying them – loudly and softly, slowed down and speeded up – until eventually (we were both sweating with the strain) he succeeded in making out 'the Benešov' road. Within minutes our News Bureau, in our presence, was on the line to RAF headquarters and to the command of the Czechoslovak airforce. But we could have saved ourselves the nervous strain. Sadly they told us they were not allowed to intervene. It had been agreed at Yalta that the liberation of Czechoslovakia was to be performed by the Soviet Union. (Some time later I wrote an account, based entirely on genuine monitored material, of *The Liberation of Prague*. This was broadcast by the BBC in English and, in an abridged form, in Czech, as well as, many years later, on several separate anniversaries of the Rising, by Prague Radio.)

PART THREE

Chapter Eight

After the War

When Mary was expecting our first child we decided to get a house near Caversham Park and Mary would give up working. The house we eventually found, and which we could afford, was an old-fashioned semi-detached house in Sonning Common, a village about three miles from my work, on a bus line to Reading with a stop near Caversham Park. There was a lot wrong with the house, but it was cheap, and we were young and confident that we could improve it. It had three floors – on the ground floor there were two rooms and the kitchen, which was in a large wooden shed roofed with corrugated iron and accessed from the back room, which would therefore be our dining room. On the first floor were two rooms and a bathroom. On the second floor, reached by a proper staircase, there were two attic rooms with sloping ceiling. These also extended in part over the house next-door, i.e., the other 'half' of the semi-detached pair. The kitchen had a door into the garden, with a kind of fuel shed just outside. And there was another, much bigger, shed at the bottom of the garden. The garden was quite large, L-shaped, embracing as it were the garden of the other semi detached house. The house had belonged to an old lady, who had clearly not done anything to it for many years. The rooms had open fireplaces. Mary's parents were horrified when they saw it: they thought we had thrown our money away. They were wrong: when we sold the house some fifteen years later – admittedly we had greatly improved it by then – we received a multiple of what we paid for it. The first thing we did was to buy stoves for our sitting and dining rooms; these worked on coal, coke or anthracite, or a mixture of these, and heated the rooms much more efficiently with rather less work than open fireplaces required and would stay in all night. Next we bought inexpensive furniture. One of our best buys, at a local auction sale – new furniture was rationed, but not second-hand – was an enormous beautiful mahogany 'gentleman's wardrobe', with hanging space in one half and a set of large open 'French' drawers in the other. I divided this piece of furniture and fitted the two halves into the chimney recesses of our bedroom. We found someone to tidy up the garden and a couple of demobilized Poles to rebuild the shed at the bottom of the garden, turning one half of it into a garage with proper garage doors. Not far from us there was a camp, during the war a camp for Italian prisoners of war, where, after the war, men of the Free Polish Army, who did not want to go back to Communist Poland, were accommodated until they found employment or, as did a lot of them, married English girls. Those two Poles did a fantastic job: not only did they work hard and efficiently, but each day when they had finished they cleaned their tools – that is, my tools – as no doubt they had done their rifles not so long before. With my Czech, and with the Lachian I had learned from translating Lysohorsky, we had no problem communicating.

Our garden contained a lot of soft fruit – strawberries, raspberries, loganberries, gooseberries, red and black currants, and, above all, cherries. There was a lot of demand for these among my colleagues at work, and some days I came to work with thirty or more pounds of 'white heart' cherries, weighed out in one-pound paper bags. There was also a big apple tree and a plum tree, an 'early Rivers' plum, but that was not very productive. Mary bottled hundreds and hundreds of pounds of soft fruit and stewed apple – fruit, even bottled fruit, was still at a premium in postwar Britain.

Our daughter Margaret was born on 21 April 1947, the birthday of The Queen. As a small girl she was always delighted to hear the National Anthem played on the radio on her birthday.

In 1948 came the Communist take-over in Czechoslovakia, the 'victorious February', and a lot of former members of the Czechoslovak army in the West returned to England. Those whose children had been born in Britain had no difficulty about readmission, but quite a few of them had to leave Czechoslovakia illegally. One of these was Lubor Zink, who had been an artillery officer in the Czechoslovak army and who was now engaged by the Monitoring Service as a Czech monitor. Although I did not share his ultra-conservative political views, we became good friends. (He later became a well-known political journalist in Canada, with several journalistic prizes to his name, as well as, after the Velvet Revolution, a number of Czech honours. Alas, he has since died.) Lubor was then a human dynamo. He took one look at our kitchen and immediately proposed how to remodel it. With timber and hardboard, we ran up a partition wall, with a swing door in it, dividing the working part from a storage area. And we painted the whole kitchen a sunny yellow. It made a vast difference. By way of return I helped him build a brick garage-shed at his house, quite close to ours. We had neither of us done any bricklaying before, but we had watched bricklayers at work and Lubor decided that any intelligent person could do it. We did. And he was right. That garage-shed still stands today, more than fifty years later. In the early summer of 1947, a few weeks after Margaret was born, my brother came to visit us in England. The reason why it took two years before we saw each other again, when for six years we did not even know if the other was still alive, was that he was for a long time refused an exit visa. And the reason for that was that he had a brother in England and might decide to stay there. He was actually told that. Apart from that he had had his bad leg broken again and reset, and for quite a while was unable to walk. He was also, understandably, like so many other concentration camp survivors, suffering from delayed shock and nightmares. We had, of course, corresponded with each other right from the start, and in 1947 we at long last saw each other again after nine years. I remember driving down to Dover to meet him off the Channel ferry. He had been through experiences which to me were quite unimaginable, but all in all he was in better shape than I had expected.

In the summer of 1948 I visited the Continent for the first time since the war. With two colleagues – Mary had to stay behind with our one-year-old daughter – I drove down through France into Haute Savoie. I had by then bought another car, a 16-year-old Talbot with a Darracq body, the most luxurious car I ever owned, but of course it was old and prone to breakdowns. Postwar Europe was then still a barter economy. I remember filling up the boot of the car with dozens of tins of food, mainly coffee, dried milk and various other goods we knew were in short supply in France. At petrol stations – they were still pumping petrol by hand – we just opened the boot and said: Fill her up and take what you think the *essence* is worth. No money changed hands, and both sides were happy. We were all three of us keen skiers and mountaineers, anxious to be among mountains again. We drove up to Chamonix, decided that this was too grand and expensive a place for us, and continued to the next village up the valley, Argentière. There, in a bar – where else in France? – we made the acquaintance of Peter Brook, who, though only just out of university, had already made a name for himself as a theatrical director, as well as of a local *moniteur de ski*, a ski instructor. When he heard that we were (or had been) keen skiers, he offered to take us up to the Col du Géant on Mont Blanc and ski with us down the Vallée Blanche. We each had a pair of British army boots, from our Home Guard days, taken along for mountain walking. Our *moniteur* adapted these for cable bindings by nailing thin strips of leather to the heels, and provided us with quite decent skis. We took the little rack railway up to the Mer de Glace and from there, carrying our skis and a rucksack, we walked up the glacier for several hours, jumping over crevasses. We spent the night in the Refuge du Requin, an extremely primitive hut with just one multisex dormitory, but we slept like logs. At four in the morning we set out, now roped up by our guide, and climbed up the steep and difficult icefall of the Glacier du Géant to the top of the 3,359 m Col. (From Courmayeur on the Italian side of Mont Blanc you can get up there effortlessly by cable car.) There we put on our skis and, somewhat gingerly, also because of the altitude, started our leisurely descent. I remember that the French skiing champion (whose name I have forgotten), who was a friend of our *moniteur*, watched us for a while and then said to him: '*Mais ils sont culottés*' [literally: they are already wearing breeches, meaning: they'll do]. It was, and even in retrospect still is, a wonderful experience to be skiing on Europe's highest mountain.

The end of the war and the emerging East-West conflict – perhaps not quite yet the Cold War – had naturally resulted in changes in monitoring policy. Emphasis shifted from German broadcasts to broadcasts from the Soviet Union and the Soviet sphere of influence. From being predominantly a German monitor, right to the German surrender, I now became the chief monitor, i.e., the head, of the Czech team of monitors.

Like many of us in the Monitoring Service I had, on the whole, viewed my employment as a form of war service and was wondering if I now had a future in it. So when the Allied Control Commission advertised for translator/interpreters I thought I might at least apply and take the tests. I sat a German-into-English and English-into-German translation test at Lancaster House, a government building in London. The test was by no means easy, but the fact that, as a monitor, I had for many years been familiar with official German texts helped me a lot, especially in translating a weather report into German. Anyway, I must have done well, because within a very few days I was invited to an interview and offered the post of a 'senior translator' with the notional rank and the privileges of an army major. (Ordinary 'translators' only had the rank of captain.) It should be remembered that, in the immediate postwar period with its severe shortages, official appointments, especially abroad, were exceedingly desirable. I said that I would accept on two conditions – that I could have my wife with me, and that I was posted to Vienna and not to Germany. This the Control Commission was unable to guarantee, and so, with not too many regrets, I withdrew my application. That was before our daughter was born.

Some time later I had not exactly an offer but an unofficial approach from a wartime colleague, Stephen Ullmann – strictly speaking Baron Stephen de Ullmann, though he never used his title – to join his department of linguistics at the University of Leeds, but while this seemed attractive in a way, I was by then a paterfamilias and reluctant to abandon the relative security of the BBC for an uncertain academic future. In 1951 our son Richard was born.

In 1949 my brother again visited us in England, this time with his new Czech wife Eva, from whom he has now been separated for a number of years and more recently, divorced. I have no particular recollection of this visit, except that, officially, they had come to the UK '*na brigádu*', to do voluntary work, and soon went off to Scotland.

It is possible that the growing East-West tension had something to do with a renewed interest by British publishers in Czech writing. At any rate, about four years after *The Problems of Lieutenant Knap* I was asked by John Lehmann to translate a new book by Jiří Mucha, *Scorched Crop* [*Spálená setba*]; this was published in 1949. A few years later another publisher, Secker & Warburg, with whom I had had no connections before, approached me with an offer to translate a novel by Egon Hostovský, *Missing* [*Nezvěstný*]. This was published in London in 1952, the same year also in America, by Viking Press, and the following year as a Bantam Book paperback in New York. More and more of my translations of poetry, Czech and German, were by then appearing in literary periodicals.

For some time I was also a fairly frequent contributor to *Dial-a-Poem*. This was an enterprising scheme of the cultural department of Camden

Borough Council, the part of London where the British Museum is located. Anyone in Britain could simply dial a London telephone number and hear a recording of a few poems, usually by the same author. I do not remember how I came to be associated with this: I must have been invited by someone who had seen my translations in literary magazines. The arrangements were exceedingly primitive. No broadcast studio, just an ordinary telephone on a desk in an ordinary room on an upper floor of an ordinary house, connected to a recording machine. The producer first said a few words about the poet and, if it applied, the translator; he then simply passed the telephone to the speaker who read the poems into the mouthpiece. The poems were changed every week, the programme being published in some of the weeklies specializing on London entertainment, such as *Time Out*. I must have read on this service at least half a dozen times, usually translations of Czech poems, but later, at the suggestion of the producer, also some of my own poetry. On one occasion I brought the East German poet Reiner Kunze along during one of his rare visits to England.

In the late fifties an evening class in woodworking was started up at our village elementary school. This was not the kind of leisurely amateur class with cups of tea or coffee, but a thoroughly professional class to the syllabus of the London City & Guilds, with proper examinations at the end of the year's course. I attended for three years and became a perfectly competent carpenter and furniture maker. With these new skills I set about improving our house: I ran up a partition in our back attic, with a proper door, of course, turning one large room into two of a more practical size, I built a traditional woodworker's workbench at the far end of our garage, I made a new gate into our garden, I made a small mahogany table, a mahogany record player case, a beech and mahogany bench to match a couple of Heal's chairs, I made a pair of nesting beds for my children – the smaller one rolling under the larger one for extra space in daytime – and I framed many of the old prints of Prague which by then I had begun to collect. Most importantly, I greatly enjoyed woodwork: it seemed to me the ideal counterweight to intellectual activity.

There is a temptation, when one is looking back on a happy and moderately successful life, to put major and minor tragedies out of one's mind. But that does not mean that they were not there. For me, the greatest tragedy was the death of my mother in 1942, although I only learnt about it after the war. As my brother established, she was deported by what the Germans called the *Rachetransport*, the 'vengeance deportation', that followed the assassination of the Nazi *Reichsprotektor* Heydrich. For a long time it was believed that this train never got to Auschwitz, but was set on fire by the Germans en route. I tried to persuade myself over the years that this might have been a better way of dying than the gas chamber – but I never quite convinced myself. More recently, in 2002, a letter was discovered from a person on that transport, from which it appeared that the train actually reached a place called Ujazdów. Some of the deportees were there at first employed on digging trenches. It is thought that they were then sent to the extermination camp of Sobibor. There are no survivors of that transport.

Of course I had done what, at the time, seemed to me the very best I could do to get her out of Nazi-occupied Czechoslovakia – but who can tell if I could not have tried even harder and perhaps succeeded. I am aware that all survivors have a guilt complex, more especially those who lost their dear ones in the Holocaust, but rational reflection does not help a lot.

The worst blow for my wife was the death of her younger sister Jean in an accident with a gas fire: while away from home to attend an examiners' meeting in Cambridge she had fallen asleep while gas was escaping from a presumably faulty tap. She had had a very happy marriage and left two small children. Fortunately Peter's – her husband's – mother immediately came to look after the children. Mary's other sister's husband, Frank – now also sadly dead – and I had the terrible task of driving over to Cambridge to formally identify Jean's body.

Another family tragedy struck when Mary developed multiple sclerosis. Luckily, at least, she was by then in her forties – the disease progresses much more rapidly in younger persons. At first, although there were bad days as well as good ones, we did not greatly change our lifestyle. We had, some time previously, bought a plot of land in Sonning Common with a view to having a house built for us, and we now had to get our architect to change his original plan for a two-level house to a bungalow, with doors wide enough to allow the passage of a wheelchair, in case this became necessary in the future. We continued to go on camping holidays, now with a small caravan instead of a tent, and I had been taught to administer a daily injection of ACTH. (Mary could not bring herself to use a hypodermic on herself.) From Dutch friends we had heard about a doctor in Germany, who specialized in MS and had developed an unorthodox form of treatment. We went to see him at his special clinic at Hachen in the Sauerland. His treatment consisted of the avoidance of all cooked food, in fact of any food heated above blood temperature, with the exception of bread (which was allowed), and in the avoidance of hot baths or showers. From then on, and ever since, Mary has had a cold shower every morning, even in winter, and she is convinced that this has helped to stop the advance of the disease. Over the first few years – though she has stopped doing this now – she also germinated wheat and rye seed, and ate the young shoots when they were about a quarter of an inch long. Fortunately her MS has been in remission for many years now, though of course her progressive lack of mobility, as well as advancing age, has led to a marked weakening of her muscles and she can now only walk short distances – and no steps – with the aid of a Zimmer frame.

A great shock for both of us was when our daughter Margaret, at about twelve, was knocked down in the street by a car, as she was running from school to catch a bus. It was clearly her fault, and she was exceedingly lucky. She was taken to hospital by ambulance, where they diagnosed a fracture of her pelvis, but fortunately no internal injuries. She was kept in hospital for some six weeks, with one leg on traction, and I would go down to visit her and do Latin and Mathematics with her. In the meantime I redecorated her room a cheerful yellow. She managed quite skilfully on crutches, and the accident has had no undesirable consequences of any sort.

A few years later, while she was at university in Sheffield, we paid her a tragicomical visit: Mary had had a fall in our garden and broken her ankle and our son Richard had broken his collar-bone playing rugby at school. And so, having booked ground-floor rooms in a Sheffield hotel, we arrived like a transport from the battlefield – Mary with her leg in plaster and Richard with his arm in a sling.

Although I had long ceased writing anything in German, there was just one occasion, in the early fifties, when I briefly reverted to it. I decided to translate T.S. Eliot's verse play *Murder in the Cathedral*. To my astonishment I found that I had not quite lost my ability and, after working on this translation for a few weeks, I was rather pleased with the result. I sent my translation to Eliot, who was a director of the publishing firm of Faber & Faber and asked him if I might call on him. He replied very amicably and so I visited him at his office. He thanked me for my translation, but said that his German was not good enough to judge it. He had therefore sent it to Ashley Dukes, the director of the Mercury Theatre, and a playwright, who would write to me. (In fact, it was Ashley Dukes who first staged *Murder in the Cathedral* in 1935.) I visited T.S. Eliot once more, I do not remember exactly why, and we exchanged some letters about *Murder in the Cathedral*. (My correspondence with him, as well as my German translation of his verse play, is now in the archives of the British Library.) Eliot has often been accused of anti-Semitism. There are indeed a few anti-Jewish remarks in his poetry, but I would like to put it on record that, although of course he must have known that I had come to England as a Jewish refugee, he was perfectly courteous and charming to me. I soon heard from Ashley Dukes, who was by then in charge of cultural affairs under the Allied Control Commission in Germany. He was most complimentary about my translation and on the spot offered me a contract for two performances in Germany, at what seemed to me a very attractive fee. I was over the moon. A few weeks later, however, I received another letter from him. It had been discovered that the German poet Rudolf Alexander Schröder had translated Eliot's play a few years previously and registered his translation in the US Library of Congress. The law therefore required the Control Commission to stage his translation and not mine. It was one of my greatest literary disappointments: to have been Eliot's translator – or even one of his translators – moreover with two public performances of my translation, would have been quite something. I have had a thorough look at Schröder's translation and honesty compels me to admit that it is rather good. Some sections, I felt, were better in his version than in mine, but others were better in my translation. At least I was consoled by the fact that I so nearly got there and was defeated only by a legal technicality. A short while later, Martin Esslin, who had been a colleague in the Monitoring Service under his original name of Pereszlenyi, and who was by then Head of Radio Drama, considered broadcasting my translation of *Murder in the Cathedral*, but somehow this did not eventually come off. Sadly, he developed Parkinson's and died a few years ago.

At the BBC meanwhile I had been moved – perhaps promoted – to the Editorial Department and, because I had a degree in Russian, assigned to the Russian Desk. There were five 'desks' – The Soviet Union, Eastern Europe, Western Europe, Africa, The Far East. Each of these desks produced a daily 'Summary of World Broadcasts' by selecting significant monitored material, condensing it to about one-tenth of its original length and presenting it in a readily readable form for busy civil servants. (Now that the war was over the material produced by the Monitoring Service also went to a large number of paying subscribers in Britain and abroad, such as newspapers, news agencies, etc.) Soon it was decided that the Russian Desk should, in addition, produce a 'Weekly Summary of Soviet Economic Affairs' for the Economic Intelligence Unit of the British Ministry of Defence – and I was appointed to be the editor of this new weekly publication. There was a huge amount of economic news broadcast by Moscow and other Soviet stations and put out by the Tass agency. Before long I was quite an expert on Soviet geography and on the progress of the many dams, reservoirs and 'nature-changing' projects. In my new capacity, along with the head of my department, I repeatedly had to visit some of our governmental clients, such as the Economic Intelligence unit of the Ministry of Defence. Their interests were highly specialized and, most of the time, exceeded the facilities of the Monitoring Service ('What we want to know is what ship the Soviets are presently building in the No.2 dry dock in Nikolaev'). Even so they assured us that quite often they found a nugget in our monitored material.

At the beginning of 1962, when I had worked in the Monitoring Service for nearly twenty-three years, the BBC decided, as a 'change of air', to send me for two or three months 'on attachment' to the Russian section of the European Service in London. This was an exciting challenge. It meant a train journey of a little over an hour to Waterloo Station, from where I walked over Waterloo Bridge to Bush House, a walk of about ten minutes and in fine weather a very enjoyable one. The head of the Russian section was Prince Alexander Lieven, a charming man with an absolutely perfect command of English, Russian, German and French. We got on very well together. The rest of the section's staff were a mixture of native Russian and English speakers: the news bulletins were invariably read by native Russians, but commentaries were occasionally given by non-Russians, who of course spoke Russian fluently. One of my first duties was to write a daily review of the British press, to be written by me in English for translation by some of the native Russians. This worked very well. I used to buy four or five papers at Reading Station before getting on my train, read the lead stories and editorials on my journey, making a few notes, so that the press review was virtually ready in my head when I got to the office. Technically I was a 'producer': I would compile news bulletins from the material supplied in English by the News Room, making the selection with an eye to a Russian audience and fitting it into however many minutes I was told were available. I also sat in the control room of the studio during broadcasts, composed letters to celebrities we were hoping to interview and made myself generally useful. It was an interesting experience.

When I returned from my 'attachment' in London I was made a 'chief report writer' and put in charge of the Eastern Europe Desk, which of course included Czechoslovakia. In addition to running my team of five or six report writers and assigning their specific work to them, it was my duty to write a one-page analysis of the contents of the daily Summary for those clients who were too busy to read its entire fifteen to twenty pages. I held this post until 1970.

But it was in the late fifties and the early sixties that my literary translation work got into full stride. (This was, of course, then a part-time activity as I was still working in the Monitoring Service.) I was approached by Joe Gaute of Harraps with an invitation to translate several novels by the then fashionable and successful German author Hans Habe. Thus my first translation from the German, *Off Limits*, appeared in 1956, and the same year in New York, and as a paperback in 1958. This was followed by Hans Habe's *All My Sins* in 1958, and by his hugely successful *Agent of the Devil*, also in 1958. This book appeared in the USA as *The Devil's Agent* in the same year and, republished in paperback, in 1959 and again in 1968, 1969 and 1973. I had by then become something of a 'house translator' for Harraps, with whom I had a very amicable and good relationship for many years, translating another sixteen books for this publisher.

However, my first step towards fame as a translator – if indeed there is such a thing – came when I was commissioned by Collins to translate, together with my colleague and friend Hanns Hammelmann, a major 'important' book – *The Correspondence between Richard Strauss and Hugo von Hofmannsthal*. To ensure that the two 'voices' were preserved also in translation, it was decided that Hanns Hammelmann should do Hofmannsthal's letters, while I would do Strauss's. This seemingly simple division of labour in fact involved a great deal of work. Since each letter-writer in answering the other took up the actual phrases used by the other, we had to collaborate all the time. But it was fascinating work. When the translation came out in 1961 it received a four-page review in the *Times Literary Supplement* by none less than W.H. Auden, and when, many years later, I was on a reading tour of American universities, I discovered that I was known everywhere as the translator (or co-translator) of this book. It has repeatedly been republished on both sides of the Atlantic, and excerpts from the correspondence were broadcast and often quoted in opera programmes.

The intensification of the Cold War in the 1950s made life more difficult for my brother in Prague. Having graduated from the new College of Economics and Politics he was working as a journalist on the staff of *Lidové Noviny*: hence having a brother in the BBC Monitoring Service, regarded by the Communists as an espionage organization, was distinctly unhelpful. Conversely, though to a lesser, and far less dangerous, degree having a Communist journalist as a brother, was not exactly an ideal situation for me either. At one point, when my duties included writing a special daily political abstract for Sir Robert Bruce-Lockhart, for use in his broadcasts to Czechoslovakia, I found that his arguments specifically, and by name, targeted some articles written by my brother. (Sir Robert did not know the identity of the provider of his material.)

1952 was the year of the political show trials in Czechoslovakia. Throughout Stalin's empire a fierce campaign sprang up against Jews in key positions in the state and in the Party: they were seen as rootless 'cosmopolitans' without loyalty to any country, as subversive elements, and as American spies. In the first political trial in Prague eleven high-ranking figures were sentenced to death and at the beginning of December 1952 hanged. One of them, Vladislav Clementis, I knew quite well in London during the war. He was then the highest-ranking Slovak in Beneš's government-in-exile. Eduard Goldstücker, until then Czechoslovak ambassador to Israel, was arrested in a second wave, imprisoned at the Secret Police prison in Ruzyně, 'prepared for trial' for over a year, and eventually sentenced to life imprisonment. My brother thinks he was comparatively lucky to have only been sacked from the newspaper, stripped of his degree, and made to work as a storekeeper at the ČKD factory. This might not have happened to him if I had had a different job in England.

Before the war we had owned a house in Munich – I do not really know how this came about. It stood in a good position, along the Isar river, but it had been totally destroyed in an Allied air raid. However, with the help of a lawyer in London, I managed to sell the ruin, and the proceeds were just about enough for my brother in Prague to buy himself a second-hand car with half the money.

In 1965 I decided to visit Prague with my whole family and to camp in Czechoslovakia. We were towing a small caravan. We drove across Germany and crossed the frontier near Cheb. It was at the frontier that we had the first Švejk-type experience. The customs guard sternly informed me that he had to inspect the inside of the caravan. So I produced my key and we both stepped inside. As soon as I had shut the door behind us he said: 'Let's waste no time. What should I do to get my son to England? Into some school or into a family?' I do not think my answer was very helpful, but we were allowed to pass. Cheb was in a mess, but Karlovy Vary seemed just as before the war. On the way to Prague we stopped at one of the infrequent petrol stations. Did I know, the attendant asked me, that Lány, with 'the president's grave', was quite close? He meant, of course, T.G. Masaryk – but he had died some thirty years previously and the country had since had two other presidents, three if you count Hácha. I found this rather touching. We had planned to stay at the Bráník camp ground in Prague. On the way into the city I asked a tram pointsman the way. He smiled at me and said: 'Nothing's changed here. You drive exactly the same way as you'd have done before the war.' And he was right. It was dead easy.

In the 1960s began a long-lasting and enjoyable relationship with a Swiss publisher, the geographical publishing house Kümmerly & Frey in Bern. Originally publishers of maps and atlases, they had recently embarked on the production of beautiful large colour-plate books. The photographs, which were of outstanding quality, were accompanied by a text describing the landscape and the political and economic conditions of the country concerned. These covered *The Aegean World, The Sahara, Spitsbergen, The Camargue, The Grand Canyon, Iceland, Denmark, Sweden, Norway*, and a few others. In the seventies the firm also asked me to translate some of their new series of pocket guides (India, Ceylon, Bali). This was not strictly literary translation, but the books were very attractive and I enjoyed the work.

All the time that I was doing these book translations, for which of course I was being paid, I also translated a great number of Czech poems for publication (usually unpaid) in literary periodicals. I was a regular contributor to *Modern Poetry in Translation* (edited then by Daniel Weissbort and Ted Hughes), to *London Magazine* (edited by Alan Ross), to *Outposts* (edited by Howard Sargeant) – these three in England – and to *Contemporary Literature in Translation* in Vancouver, Canada, as well as being an occasional contributor to several others. Alan Ross, who sadly died in 2001, in particular invited me to submit translated poetry and later sent me other translators' volumes of poetry to review.

Howard Sargeant went even further. He urged me to write my own poetry in English: my translations of foreign poetry had convinced him, he said, that I was now ready to write poetry in English. I had, in point of fact, not written any poetry since 1939, when I stopped writing in German. For something like twenty-five years I had been without what is, rather bombastically, called a 'creative language'. English, admittedly, had become my instinctive language, almost a second mother tongue – even though I never lost my foreign accent – but somehow it seemed to me that to write my own poetry in English would nevertheless be something very different from translating poetry into English. The person who really 'loosened my tongue' was John Lehmann. I clearly remember the moment. I was visiting him at his flat in Earls Court and I was complaining to him that I was, linguistically, between two stools. I had lost German as a creative language and I did not feel I could write my own stuff in English. 'Why the hell not?' Lehmann said almost angrily. 'Joseph Conrad did it and Arthur Koestler is doing it right now.' That was the defining moment. I do not believe that posterity will be especially grateful to John Lehmann for having made me write poetry in English, but personally I owe him a great debt of gratitude.

I began to write poetry, I found it was accepted in English literary magazines, and one of my poems actually came second in a competition. In 1971 my first (very slim) volume appeared in a small publishing house, and one reviewer actually said that a lot of contemporary English poets would be glad to handle English with such easy assurance as this foreign-born Ewald Osers did with what for him was an acquired language. I almost burst with pride.

In the early sixties Jiří Mucha, of whom it had been said by some that he had accommodated himself with the Communist regime, found himself arrested and sentenced to work in the uranium mines in northern Bohemia. While there, he had kept a secret diary, its individual pages being smuggled out by a sympathetic prison warder. When he was eventually discharged he wrote what I believe was his most powerful book, *Studené slunce*, which in my English translation has the title *Living and Partly Living* – a quotation from T.S. Eliot. It came out in England in 1967 and in the United States in 1968.

In the sixties I was a member of the Labour Party – even, in a small way, what might be called an activist. Before elections I went canvassing, during elections I drove elderly supporters to the polling station and acted as 'teller' by the door, ticking off the names of those who came out after voting. But I resigned from the party, as did Mary, in 1968, when it failed to condemn the entry of the Warsaw Treaty armies into Czechoslovakia. I well remember, at a meeting of my local party, hearing a local official declaring that the Soviet Union probably had good reason to stop the 'counter-revolution' of the 'Prague Spring'. I demonstratively walked out of the meeting and addressed a letter of resignation to the party as soon as I got home. I think for the next few elections we voted Liberal. When the 'Gang of Four' – Roy Jenkins, Shirley Williams, David Owen and Will Rodgers – left the party in 1981 to form the Social Democratic Party my sympathies were with them. And when, in the course of time, the Liberal Democratic Party was created, in 1988, we became founder members and continue, in a small way, to contribute to its funds. One of the reasons that attract me to it is that its programme calls for higher taxation, at least on the better-off, in order to finance the necessary investments in education and health. The other parties, of course, know that these investments are impossible without higher taxation, but, for vote-catching reasons, avoid admitting it.

The Soviet-led invasion of Czechoslovakia in 1968, to stifle the efforts of the 'reform Communists' to create 'socialism with a human face', was one of the greatest challenges to the Monitoring Service – mainly because the regular broadcasting networks broke down as the invaders captured the transmitters, and unscheduled broadcasting went out from a multiplicity of small transmitters (ironically enough, set up by the Communist Party for the event of a popular uprising). Every single Czech monitor was brought in – there were no days off – I myself was 'brought down' from Editorial to do some monitoring, after which I changed roles and went upstairs to my Eastern Europe desk to process the monitored Czech material. Monitors of related languages (Polish, Serbo-Croat) were 'borrowed' to watch stations and to call out for a Czech monitor when it seemed that an announcement might be made. On the day after the invasion BBC Television teams arrived at Caversham Park and I, as the most senior Czech monitor, was interviewed to camera on my analysis of the events of the past few hours. I thus appeared on national television three days running, as well as on radio – a fact that was not missed on 'the other side'. (I shall come back to this later.)

I had by then translated a lot of Nezval's poems from his surrealist volume *Prague with Rain Fingers*, as well as poems by Antonín Bartušek – a poet not actually banned but sidelined by the Communists because of his Catholicism – and by Josef Hanzlík. I succeeded in persuading Nikos Stangos, then at Penguin, to bring out a Czech volume in that firm's new *Modern European Poetry* series. This appeared in 1970 under the title *Three Czech Poets: Nezval, Bartušek, Hanzlík*. Being a Penguin paperback, it was published in a vastly greater print-run than any of my previous volumes. It cost the even then ludicrously small sum of 5 shillings – 25 new pence – but has since become a collector's piece and is offered at a high price on the internet.

Bartušek and I became friends. When he visited England with his wife and daughter they stayed for a night or two at our house. And in 1975 his *Aztec Calendar*, a very powerful cycle of poems, appeared in my translation with Anvil Press, then a new and small publishing house but now one of the leading firms for poetry.

As more books began to be published with my name on them as the translator, it was suggested to me that I join the newly set up Translators Association, a daughter organization of the Society of Authors. I did so and a few years later, in 1971, I was elected its chairman. (Subsequently I had two more periods in the chair, both of them for two years, 1980-81 and 1983-84.)

In 1971 I won my first translation prize – the Schlegel-Tieck Prize for the best translation of a German book during the year under review – Paul Carrell's account of the German attack on the Soviet Union. The prize was presented to me, together with a cheque, by the German ambassador, at a splendid reception. Moreover – this does not unfortunately apply any longer – the prize then included a week's visit to the Federal Republic of Germany as an official guest.

This was a Walter Mitty-ish experience. As I got off the plane at Bonn/Cologne airport and presented my passport, the official said: 'You're being expected,' took me out of the line and handed me to a gentleman and a lady from the German foreign office. An official car was waiting outside, with a uniformed driver, and I was driven to the Hotel Königshof. To my astonishment I found the entrance drive lined by soldiers with tommy-guns. 'Don't worry,' I was told. 'They're not for you. The Jordanian foreign minister is also staying at the hotel.' I had been able to choose the places I wanted to go to, and had chosen those where German poets were living whose work I was interested in, and had partly been translating. After Cologne and Bonn, where I was escorted by a gentleman from the foreign ministry, I travelled to Munich, where I was met off the train by Count Keyserlinck (who has since embraced Buddhism and adopted an Indian name), who accompanied me to Radio Free Europe. I then travelled by train to Münster, where I wanted to meet Hans-Dieter Schäfer, a volume of whose 'prose poems', *Strawberries in December*, appeared in my translation several years later, in 1976, with Carcanet Press. From Münster, a very interesting town, where the Westphalian Peace which ended the Thirty Years' War was signed in 1648, I travelled by a wonderful modern train to Kiel, to stay with another poet I had worked on, Hans-Jürgen Heise (my volume *Underseas Possessions* appeared with Oleander Press in 1972). From there I returned to Hamburg, where I visited Paul Carell, the author of the book whose translation had won me the Schlegel-Tieck Prize, and the Czech humorist writer Gabriel Laub, who was a good friend of my brother's. My next (and final) venue was Berlin, where I was taken over by a lady who represented InterNationes there. I was taken to the new Berlin opera house for a splendid performance of *Cavalleria Rusticana* and *Pagliacci*, I was taken to one of those observation platforms from which one could see over the Berlin Wall, and finally – without the InterNationes lady, who was not allowed to enter the Soviet-controlled German Democratic Republic – was put on a sightseeing bus via the famous (or notorious) Checkpoint Charlie into East Berlin. This outing was of no great interest: the bus tour went first to the Soviet war memorial, which consisted of sixteen identical monuments, one for each of the sixteen Soviet republics, and then to the Hotel Berolina, where it was hoped that the Western visitors would spend some hard currency in its privileged hard-currency shop. From Berlin I flew home. The whole visit had been enormously generous – I was put up in the most expensive hotels everywhere, taken to the best restaurants, and was generally made a great deal of fuss of.

As I have mentioned before, in the early sixties Mary had been diagnosed with multiple sclerosis. We had by then decided to move out of our inconvenient house and have a new house built for us on a plot that Mary had discovered – it had a temporary building on it the permit for which had expired and which had to be pulled down anyway. We had chosen a young architect whose work we liked, and, as I have said, he had already prepared the plans for a two-story house, when, in view of Mary's MS, we realized that we would have to have a bungalow. To save on building costs, and to make sure that our future home would be suitable for a disabled person – none of us could tell at the time how badly affected Mary would be – I decided to do the entire electrical installation myself. (Not, however, our electrical underfloor heating, which required the laying of cables into the wet concrete floor.) I read up the rules, studied installation manuals, and planned the electrical outlets so that, no matter what appliances we would have in the future, there would never be a need for a cable to run across the floor. Using exclusively double-outlet sockets, I finished up with a total of 92 outlets in the house – not counting the separate heavy-ampère outlets for the cooker and water heater. I went to the site every day while building was going on and arranged my annual leave to coincide with the time when the walls and ceilings were up, but before they were plastered. I bought a few professional tools for wire-stripping, I paid a teenage lad from the village to help me with the chiselling-out of the recesses for junction boxes, sockets and switches, but I myself did all the actual wiring. The small hardware and electrical shop in the village was most cooperative: they supplied all the different cabling, the fuse-boxes, the main switches, etc., at wholesale prices. I had spent what in retrospect seems a ridiculous amount of time choosing attractive socket covers, switches and multiple switches – in our living/dining room we have two banks of quadruple switches – and by working very hard and long hours I got our well-above-average electrics installed without holding the builders up. Naturally, since I was not a qualified electrician, the whole installation had to be thoroughly tested by the Electricity Board, but my work passed all tests.

Applying my woodwork skills I also designed and made all our sliding-door kitchen cupboards – none of the makes on the market met all my demands – and, with the help of a young man from a Reading do-it-yourself shop, built an elaborate cupboard arrangement with access from the kitchen for crockery storage and access from the dining area to a drinks cabinet. I also designed and assembled a room divider unit with space for a television set and, from the other side, a shelf for a record-player that I bought for my Schlegel-Tieck Prize money but which is no longer in use. I also designed a 'floating' multiple light fitting for our sitting room, but this had to be manufactured (to my specifications) in a furniture workshop.

Chapter Nine

America and Italy

In 1964 we moved into our new house and in the autumn of that year I also made my first trip to America. After twenty-five years of apparently satisfactory service the BBC gave me two months' paid leave, together with a small sum of money, on condition that this was used for 'broadening my horizon'. I decided to use it for touring as much of the United States as possible. I had friends from Prague at various points along the Eastern seaboard and also in California, but I had no one I knew in the interior of the continent. Nevertheless I planned my route, as far as possible, from friend to friend (or from friend to friend's friend), and got a small Reading travel agent, who really entered into the spirit of my plan, to find me the cheapest travel. He came up with flying out to New York via Iceland, by Icelandic airline Loftleidir, travelling within the USA by Greyhound – they were offering a ludicrously cheap go-anywhere ticket valid for thirty days – and returning from Fort Lauderdale, Florida, by a New Zealand ship, the *Ruahine*, on which he booked me a berth in a four-person cabin. As soon as I had my Icelandic air ticket, the airline came up with a special offer of spending a day in Reykjavik for a promotional charge of £2 – which, admittedly, was then worth rather more than it is today. Anyway, I took it up. The hotel was excellent, so was the food, and the offer included a sightseeing bus tour (which I took), a swim in a geyser-heated open-air pool (which I did not take; after all this was late October), a visit to the Icelandic parliament (which I took), a visit to the workshop of Iceland's most famous sculptor (which I took, but could have done without), and a voucher for free entry plus two drinks at a local nightclub (which was closed that day). I am glad I spent the twenty-four hours in Iceland. On the day after my arrival I flew on to New York by the same plane. In New York I was put up by the son-in-law of a distant relation of my father's – I had not met him or his wife before, but they were most hospitable. In Philadelphia I stayed for a couple or three days with good friends – she was a classmate in Prague and he was three years above me at school – who took me to see the largest collection of Renoir paintings in the world and, moreover, arranged that another (less close) friend from Prague, who was high up in the World Bank, would drive me to Washington and put me up at his house. On the following morning I went along with him to the polling station: it was the presidential election that brought victory to Johnson. From Washington, which I liked a lot (and still do) I returned to New York and boarded a Greyhound bus going West. For economy reasons I chose night rides, to save the cost of hotel nights. My next major stop was Chicago, but I did not see very much of the city, certainly not the attractive area by the lake that I saw many years later.

It is not until you travel across the USA on the ground that you realize the enormous size of it. Denver, Colorado, was the first place I had to spend a night in a hotel, but my taxi driver from the Greyhound terminal took me to a very cheap one, my room only cost 5 dollars. I remember a stop at Reno, Nevada, the gambling state, where the Greyhound station was equipped with dozens of one-arm-bandit gambling machines. The most wonderful part of my four-day east-to-west ride was the crossing of the Rocky Mountains, by the historical Donner trail. There was snow all round, brilliant sunshine from a blue sky, and, although it was very early in the season, a few skiers. Then came Sacramento, the state capital of California, and on to San Francisco. There I was put up by the friend of a friend, a professor of German, who gave a party for me that included the translator of Christian Morgenstern. He also arranged for a radio interview on a local station. His wife drove me over the Golden Gate bridge to Sonoma, where I saw giant redwoods for the first time in my life. I also visited the Berkeley campus and stood in front of Shore Hall on the historic day of the beginning of the great student revolt. My host had also arranged for me to give a talk to the students at San José, who had their own radio station and were interested to hear about anti-Communist radios in Europe, such as Radio Free Europe and the Voice of America. It was the first of many times that I addressed American students.

From San Francisco I continued to Los Angeles. There two friends from Prague put me up in their luxurious house in Beverly Hills, right among the mansions of the film stars. My next stop was New Orleans, which I found quite fascinating, even though, because of the humid heat, I had to go back to my hotel three times during the morning to change my shirt. In the evening I strolled through the French Quarter, through the mainly open-air strip joints, and spent some time listening to genuine improvised New Orleans jazz. After that I went to Jacksonville, in Florida, where I stayed with a classmate and her husband. They drove me to St. Augustine, the scene of a recent earthquake. with a lot of wrecked and badly damaged houses. But the 200-year-old fort, built against the Seminole Indians, was quite undamaged. The son of my Jacksonville hosts lived in Miami, and that was my next stop. He had arranged for me to be accommodated in an inexpensive hotel on Miami Beach, and I remember – perhaps out of bravado – walking into the ocean for a brief (and rather cold) swim. By then it was December, but of course this was southern Florida.

A few days later I went to Fort Lauderdale to board the *Ruahine*. This New Zealand ship already had some two hundred passengers on board, most of them, as I later learned, New Zealand teachers going to England under an exchange scheme, and there were only four or five people embarking at Fort Lauderdale. Having a berth in a four-berth cabin worked out surprisingly well. My three cabin mates were men in their twenties, who spent the whole night in the bar and only returned to the cabin as, or even after, I was getting up. Then they slept all day and were back in the bar by the time I went to bed. It was almost as good as having a cabin to myself. The five-day crossing to England was rather boring, but I did a lot of walking round the deck and I swam in the ship's pool, which was filled from the sea, so long as the water was of a tolerable temperature. All in all, my 'sabbatical' two months were a most interesting experience and had given me a good idea of America.

In the early seventies my attention was drawn to Reiner Kunze, a young poet in East Germany living under continual harassment by the regime. I wrote to him, and to his great surprise my letter actually got through to him. We began a fairly intensive correspondence – our letters always got through but I have no doubt that they were read and probably copied by the Stasi, the Security Police of the German Democratic Republic. I began to translate his poetry and in 1973 had *With the Volume Turned Down* published by London Magazine Editions in London. When the Bavarian Academy of Fine Arts awarded him its Great Literature Prize and he went to Munich to receive it, along with his Czech wife – the regime made sure of their return by not allowing their young daughter to travel with them – the Bavarian Academy invited me as his translator to attend the ceremony, and we finally met in person. (On that occasion I was astonished to find that all the speeches began with '*Königliche Hoheit*' – 'Your Royal Highness' – the Highness apparently being Princess Louise, the widow of Alfred Prince of Bavaria, a cousin of the last king. Half a century after the abdication of King Ludwig III in 1918 the royalist-minded Bavarians were still paying their respects to the old lady in the front row of the auditorium. She probably held some honorary position on the Board of the Academy.)

Several years later, in 1978, my translation of *The Lovely Years*, a collection of short prose pieces, was published in London. Kunze continued to get into conflict with the Communist authorities, but his international reputation by then was such that they were reluctant to take drastic action against him. In the end they put him before the alternative of leaving the country or being arrested and tried. Like many other East German writers he moved to the Federal Republic. While he was settled in the West, he and Rolf-Dieter Brinkmann were invited to England for a reading tour, which came to a shocking end when Brinkmann was run over and killed by a London bus. A few days earlier Reiner Kunze had stayed at our house, and after the tragedy he stayed with Michael Hamburger in East Anglia.

In 1971 – as mentioned earlier – Tom Maschler, the director of Jonathan Cape and himself originally a refugee from Germany, agreed to publish my *Selected Poems* by Ondra Lysohorsky. The volume, which came out the same year with Grossmann Publishers in New York, in addition to my 56 translations, also contained seven translations made by W. H. Auden and Isobel Levitin, ten by Hugh McKinley, and two by Lydia Pasternak-Slater, the sister of Boris Pasternak. I had some correspondence with Auden in connection with this book, but in a fit of generosity I donated the letters to be auctioned for a literary charity; they were sold by Quaritch, who have refused to disclose the identity or location of their present owner.

From about 1960 on I became a regular skier again, spending two weeks in the Austrian Tyrol each year. A few times I went with a party from Erna Low – a wartime colleague who had set up a successful travel agency for keen (but expense-conscious) skiers. On two or three occasions she actually made me the leader of the party, which meant a considerable discount. I was lucky, the groups I led were no trouble at all, and nothing, fortunately, went wrong. If, as might very easily have happened, somebody had broken a leg and would have had to have been hospitalized in Austria, this might have given me a lot of trouble.

After trying several places in the Tyrol, I eventually settled for Serfaus and went there for over twenty years, always to the same Pension, indeed the same room. After ten consecutive seasons I was given a medal as an *Ehrengast*, an honoured guest, and after another ten years the mayor of the village presented me with a diploma and there were a lot of toasts. Serfaus almost became a second home to me: I knew the waiters in the restaurants, the men who operated the tow lifts, and they knew me. I became a competent skier, rising in the Austrian classification to Class II b. Class II a was better, but it was a small class with everybody being at least thirty years younger than me. Class I in most years did not exist at all; when it did, it consisted of ski instructors from Switzerland who wanted to perfect their style in Austria. On excursions from Serfaus I also skied some of the great runs in the Alps – the Piz Nair and the Diavolezza in the Engadine and – not from Serfaus but from Davos – the Parsenn.

Some time in the 1970s I was encouraged to be a member of a five-men team to represent Britain at the annual International Journalists' Ski Championships; these were held at Bayrisch Zell in southern Germany. It was an amusing, indeed a hilarious, event. Of us five 'Britons' only one was English, and the only skiing he had done was some cross-country skiing with Huskies somewhere in Scandinavia. The captain of our team was a Hungarian, George König, then there was a Vienna-born Yugoslav, Vlado Royan, the Prague-born Henry Fox (formerly Fuchs), and myself. There were teams from over fifty countries, but we all realized that we 'leisure skiers' stood no chance against such professional racing skiers as, on the Austrian team, a training partner of Toni Sailer, then world champion. But these professional racers were the 'skiing correspondents' of newspapers and therefore qualified as 'journalists' and could participate. Most of us regarded the whole event as a pleasant meeting with journalist colleagues from other countries. Only the Germans took the business deadly seriously: they had a large support team who were forever sticking thermometers into the snow at the top of the runs and further down the runs, to calculate the best kind of wax for that particular day and that particular run. Even so they did not win. The British team came near the end of the list: without our English 'hut-to-hut-with-Huskies' member we would have done a lot better, but would still have finished up well below the teams from the Alpine or Scandinavian countries.

One cannot enjoy a lifetime's skiing without coming face to face with tragedy. On one skiing holiday in Obergurgl at the top end of the Ötztal an avalanche came down a few days into our holiday, burying three or four skiers in an off-piste area. I remember the rescue team – mostly ski instructors and some locals – racing to the chair lift (which was temporarily closed to holiday skiers) in order to climb up to the site of the avalanche. They managed to get the buried skiers out alive and later in the evening, after dark – this must be a Tyrolean custom – they were skiing down with lit torches in their hands and singing.

A few days later, however, when another avalanche came down in much the same area, again burying some skiers, they were, unfortunately, only able to recover their bodies. It is difficult to describe the mood of sadness and horror that descended on the small village. Cafés and bars were either closed or, if they remained open, dispensed with their usual music. This was a depressing fortnight's skiing.

On one of my skiing holidays in Serfaus something happened to me that had never happened to me before: I was propositioned by a young woman. I do not mean encouraged – every man is occasionally encouraged or invited by a woman. I mean explicitly propositioned. This is how it happened. A small party of us, men and women, were sitting in a café, where there was dancing in the afternoon. At the neighbouring table sat a young woman who was openly staring at me. 'She wants you to dance with her,' said one of the girls in our party; 'you'd better go.' Well, why not? As soon as we were on the dance floor, she asked if I came to Serfaus every year. If I did, she would do so as well and we could have an affair. This suggestion was underlined by the way she was dancing with me. She did have a regular boy friend, she told me, but he was in a different part of Germany and they very rarely saw each other. And her gynaecologist had told her it would be bad for her health not to have sex. And if, while having sex with me, she was thinking of her boy friend, she wouldn't feel that she was being unfaithful to him. So how about it? I was a little taken aback, not shocked but faintly amused, and said to her, quite truthfully: 'When I am in bed with a woman I really like her to think of me, and not of some distant lover.' In retrospect I do not think that I have missed a lot by not accepting her offer.

On another occasion I went with a small party to have a day's skiing at Zürs-am-Arlberg, a little over an hour by bus from Serfaus and a very much more up-market centre. As we were queuing for a chair-lift an elegant car drew up alongside and out stepped the Shah of Persia with one or two personal policemen. Ordinary mortals sit down on those chair-lifts while they are (quite slowly) moving, but here the lift was stopped so that His Majesty could settle down comfortably and have a rug placed over his legs. Then the lift moved off again. Some minutes later – we were still waiting in the queue – we could see it stopping again. No doubt His Majesty had reached the top and was being helped out. We had almost forgotten about this when in the afternoon, as we were skiing down a run, an Austrian policeman on skis, in an ordinary skiing outfit but with a radio antenna sticking out of his anorak collar, made us stop, asked us to step aside, a short way off the piste, until the Shah had passed. And a minute or two later there he was – not skiing nearly as well as the members of the British royal family but inelegantly stem-swinging his way down. After a few minutes the policeman told us we could continue down. According to the local papers the Austrians were not at all pleased to have the Shah – who normally skied in St.Moritz, in Switzerland, where I had on an earlier occasion seen his private plane at the Samedan airfield – skiing in Austria this year. Europe then was full of young anti-Shah Persian students, and guarding him in the mountains, where it would have been easy enough to take a pot shot at him, must have been a nightmare for the Austrian authorities, and a rather expensive one at that.

Another slight brush, this time with a nearly-crowned head, occurred a few years later, when I was skiing with a friend from Prague – an aristocratic classmate of Edith's – at Davos. One morning she introduced me to a Frau von Habsburg, an excellent skier, whose father was an Archduke and whose grandfather, likewise an Archduke from the Brabant line of the family, was a claimant to the Spanish throne. She herself, unlike her father, was no longer a *Kaiserliche Hoheit*, an Imperial Highness, but wished to be simply addressed as Frau von Habsburg.

My only personal contact with a crowned head, admittedly one in exile, was with the King of Bulgaria, Simeon II, to whom I was presented at some reception in London as a person who translated Bulgarian poetry into English. We had quite a little chat, in Bulgarian. He seemed a very pleasant person with no side to him at all. He went back to Bulgaria, became the leader of a party called Movement for Simeon II, and, when that party came out top in the elections, became Bulgaria's prime minister under his 'civilian' name of Mr Saxe-Coburg-Gotha.

In the summer we used to go camping on the Continent with our children until they were old enough to do their own thing. We started, as did a lot of people in England, with ex-army equipment and progressed from an umbrella tent (with an awkward pole right in the middle) to an elaborate frame tent with an inner sleeping tent. When Mary's MS was diagnosed we changed from tents to a caravan which, to my retrospective amazement, we towed quite happily over Alpine passes – before the present road tunnels were built – across the southern Apennines and as far afield as Sicily. We enjoyed the camping life, which, we felt, brought us into much closer contact with the local people than hotels would.

We camped in the South of France, in the Auvergne and the Dordogne, and especially at Agde, on the Mediterranean, at a campsite owned by a Dutch couple whom I had met skiing in the Austrian Tyrol. At Agde we were joined by Otto Pick and his wife Zdenka, whom we knew before: indeed Otto Pick was at one time my subordinate at the Monitoring Service, though after the Velvet Revolution, when he returned to Prague, he made an impressive career, first as a professor at Charles University and subsequently as Deputy Minister of Foreign Affairs, at one time even First Deputy Minister.

During our stay in Agde the forest fires, which break out in the hills behind the Mediterranean coast every year, got dangerously close and one afternoon a police car with loudspeakers drove into the campsite and called on all able-bodied men to join the fire fighters. I remember how Otto Pick and I – we have since laughed about this memory – were issued with a small branch each and how with it we, rather pathetically, beat out the advancing flames. The fact that the fires did not reach the town of Agde or the campste was certainly not due to our efforts.

But most of our camping holidays were spent in Italy, which Mary and I both loved. Although we spent some time at seaside camps, both in the Gulf of Genoa and on the Adriatic coast, we mainly sought out the 'cultural' targets – Verona, Venice, Florence, Lucca, Perugia and Assisi, Siena, Urbino and Ascoli Piceno. While we loved Tuscany, we probably loved Umbria even more. In Urbino – or so we imagined – we could still feel the Renaissance civilization of which this city, under its enlightened ruler, Federico da Montefeltre (born 1422, succeeded 1444), was such an outstanding centre. We saw Viterbo with the Villa Lante, and we visited Gubbio, Montepulciano, Pienza, and of course the incomparable Orvieto on its high rock of tuff. (I had been to Orvieto before, on my Maturareise, my school-leaving trip, and a few of us were then very nearly arrested by the Carabinieri because we were rather boisterous as, more than a little drunk, we emerged from a trattoria, noisily arguing whether the cathedral was 'wine-Gothic' or 'wine-Romanesque'. On another pre-war trip to Italy a group of us teenagers went to a trattoria in Florence for an evening's wine-drinking. I remember writing on the back of the menu, in my best Italian, that we were staying in a pensione near the San Marco monastery and asking that, if we were too drunk, we should be taken there. I recall ending my request with a reminder to look *sotto la tavola*, under the table, in case one of us was lying there. In point of fact we were able to walk (or stagger) back under our own steam, except that one of us, a boy a couple of years younger than me, who carried a stack of greetings postcards we had written while still sober, instead of dropping them into a postbox was slipping them, one by one, into the private letter boxes of the houses we passed. We only realized this when it was too late. To the credit of the Florentines it should be said that most of these cards reached their addressees. (About seven or eight years later this boy, having joined the Czechoslovak airforce in Britain and been assigned to Coastal Command, sank a German U-boat and received a high decoration for this exploit.)

In central Italy, we were greatly interested in the Etruscan civilization, which preceded that of Rome. In the Civitavecchia and Tarquinia areas we visited several archaeological sites and saw a lot of Etruscan antiquities. And of course there was Rome with its overwhelming wealth of classical and Renaissance sites and, in a less hectic atmosphere, the Colli Albani with Frascati and Castel Gandolfo, and Hadrian's amazing villa and garden at Tivoli.

Perhaps I am devoting too much space here to our trips to Italy, but these were important experiences, major events in my life. I should perhaps mention here another major experience – not a Renaissance experience this time, but one from an earlier period. This was Vezelay in Burgundy, that wonderful Romanesque basilica built around 1120.

In addition to great cultural experiences there are also recollections of human kindness that stick in one's mind. In Siena – of course we should not have taken our caravan into the city centre with its narrow streets – we somehow took a wrong turn trying to get out of the city and suddenly found ourselves in a street that was getting narrower and narrower. In front of us there was a flight of steps – down which came an elegant young man in a white suit. As if this were the most natural thing in the world, he got down to helping us. There is always – there has to be – some grease in the hitch-cup and on the tow-ball, and by the time we had turned the caravan around, there were quite a few grease stains on the gentleman's white suit. We felt rather bad about this, profusely apologized and, and at Mary's suggestion, offered to pay for the suit to be cleaned. But the gentleman dismissed this, pretending to be totally unconcerned about it, and assured us how happy he was to have been able to be of help to a foreign visitor. I don't think I would have behaved in such a gentlemanly fashion had the roles been reversed. In fact, I am sure I would not.

A more bizarre thing happened to us on a camping holiday in Carinthia. Because swimming was important for Mary we had picked from our camping guide a site which had several swimming pools. One part of the campsite, behind a boarded fence, was a *Naturfreunde* site, in other words a nudist camp. As the season drew to its end, all the non-nudist pools were closed and the only way of getting our daily swim was to join the nudists. After a little hesitation we were persuaded by the camp manager's argument that we were 'all made the same way' and decided to give it a try. Seeing the 'friends of nature' nude in the water, or reclining by the pool, did not really seem too odd. The oddity began when they were engaged in non-swimming activities. Four stark naked persons sitting at a table playing bridge certainly struck one as comical, but, to my mind, the most surrealist sight was a couple – by no means particularly young or beautiful – playing table tennis, with everything on them bobbing about.

On another camping holiday, while we were in Taormina, Sicily, I received a telegram from my boss, the Head of Editorial, informing me that a senior administrative post, 'Assistant Head of Reception Department', had suddenly become vacant and asking me if I wished to be considered for it, 'Reception Unit' was the camouflage name for the department that did the actual listening-in and transcribing of foreign broadcasts. I had, for a number of years, been in Editorial and from there, from the outside, had expressed some views on how Reception Department might be run more efficiently. A move from 'operational staff' to 'management' seemed quite tempting and would also mean an appreciable rise in salary. So I replied that I wished to be considered. The Head of what would be my new department – if I got the job – was a personal friend ever since Evesham days and, indeed, is still a good friend of mine. There was some competition for the job, especially from 'inside' the department, but after a fairly gruelling interview I became 'Assistant Head of Reception Department', AHRD for short. The BBC had copied the Civil Service's traditional system of 'initials' – it was felt that initials were more professional than the use of people's names. (It also avoided the problem of whether to address a superior, whom one might know socially, by first name or surname.) Staff on 'lower management' level had only 'internal initials', which would be recognized within a service, but as a member of 'upper management' I now had 'external initials', recognized and used throughout the whole of the BBC, which at that time had a staff of some 24,000. My new duties involved, as one colleague put it, everything that HRD, my immediate boss, did not want to do himself. This was a jocular remark, but not too far from the truth. My principal task was 'quality control' of the performance of monitors. I had to devise written tests for applicants for monitors' jobs, in a form that could be evaluated in as objective a manner as possible, and I had to sit, along with my boss and the Personnel Officer, at job interviews for such applicants. In addition I had to write an annual report on each one of the then 120 monitors in the department. Writing these reports was not easy. As an enlightened employer the BBC required that each member of the staff should, at his or her 'annual interview', be shown their annual report. They were allowed to take it with them and to comment on it, or object to it, if they felt it was in any way unfair. The 'annual increment' to their salary depended on this report. I therefore had to be as frank and outspoken as possible, but whatever critical observation the report contained had to be supported by evidence that would, if necessary, stand up before arbitration. Considering that there were about three hundred working days in the year, and that I also had to take my holidays, writing 120 reports meant writing about two a week. And each of them, if one was conscientious, required looking through that particular monitor's transcripts and any notes one might have made about him or her. My new post also included a seat on the local Board of Management, which meant one meeting a week. To improve my managerial skills I was sent, on two occasions, to Upper Management Courses in a pleasant country residence, where senior public figures lectured to us and where complicated management games – including negotiation with trade union representatives – were played. I held this post for seven years, until my retirement in 1977 – retirement age throughout the BBC was sixty, both for men and women. In retrospect I have to say that I found management less enjoyable than being 'operational', though it was exceedingly interesting. Although, obviously, I tried to be as fair as possible, I did not enjoy 'playing God' and holding the future careers of what were often my former colleagues in my hands.

That was the time when the IRA staged a lot of explosions in England, often with a number of casualties and considerable damage. On one occasion, on a Saturday, when there were fewer staff in the building, we received an outside telephone call: an Irish voice warned that a bomb had been placed in the Monitoring Service building. This could have been a hoax, but our instructions were to take such warnings seriously. I happened to be the most senior person on duty – on a weekday there would have been several persons of higher rank – so I ordered the alarm to be set off and had the building evacuated. I even remembered to send a girl up to make sure there was no one left in the ladies' lavatories. BBC staff had, of course, been through fire drill before, and the building was evacuated very quickly and in an orderly fashion. There was an appointed rallying point outside, where staff would assemble after evacuation. Our alarm also rang automatically at the police station and the fire brigade. And within an impressively short time, a little over four minutes – helped, no doubt, by the lighter traffic on Saturday – the fire brigade and police had turned up. A thorough search by them did not discover any suspect package and after something like half an hour we were allowed to enter the building again. We shall never know whether this was a complete hoax or a genuine message designed, at least, to disrupt operations for a time.

At one time I was very interested in Alpine roads. One cannot drive through the Alps without, as one goes along, noticing the roads of an earlier 'generation', roads superseded by the modern ones, or here and there incorporated in them. I think that this interest was stimulated also by my collecting of old prints – I will mention this later – and of eighteenth-century steel engravings of Alpine roads. We explored a number of Alpine passes that have gone largely out of use, some of them without a modern surface, all of them narrow and often exposed – but as one hardly ever encountered another vehicle on them this did not greatly matter. (I must confess, though, that Mary did not quite share this interest of mine and that, whenever I drove along a road labelled on a Michelin map as *route dangereuse et difficile*, she would close her eyes.) I was also planning to write a book on 'Mountaineering for the Disabled' and for that purpose collected a vast number of details and prospectuses of cable-cars, small gondola lifts, and chair-lifts. I even submitted an outline of this idea to a publisher who, however, after considering it, turned it down. Besides, the Alps were then in the middle of such an explosive development, mainly for winter sport but also for summer tourism, that it would have been impossible to keep up with the development of what the brochures called 'mechanical means of ascent'. I do not want the reader of these memoirs to think that every idea I had in my life led to successful realization: there were quite a few wrong starts and blind alleys.

I became interested in old books, old maps and old engravings thanks to the encouragement of a colleague and friend, Hanns Hammelmann, a serious collector and real expert, and the author of the standard work on eighteenth-century engraved books. We used to go together to auction sales in our neighbourhood. In the first ten or fifteen years after the end of the war a lot of people were moving into smaller houses, or, in an age when domestic staff were no longer so easy or so cheap to find as between the wars, were dividing up their large homes. In consequence they got rid of a lot of what they considered clutter, including large numbers of books. A book is not simply valuable because it is old – book collecting calls for a good deal of knowledge. The fact that I worked more often on evening shift (16.00 to midnight) than on morning shift (08.00 to 16.00) made it easy to attend auction sales during the day. Not only the former owners, but also country auctioneers and even small antiquarian bookshops were astonishingly ignorant of the value of some books, and it was therefore possible to pick up real bargains. Books were usually auctioned in bundles of ten or twenty, and on some occasions I would come back from an auction sale with a few hundred books and only sort them out in our attic. If a book was really valuable, and if it was outside my special range of interest, I felt that I could not afford to keep it and therefore sold it to one of the famous rare book shops in London. On two occasions I even sold books to the British Museum – one was an early edition of Chaucer and the other was a superb binding by a binder of whom the British Museum's Keeper of Rare Books knew, but of whom until then they had no example in their collection.

After a while I decided, no doubt for sentimental reasons, to collect old maps of Bohemia and early woodcut or engraved views of Prague. These did not come up at country auction sales, but they could occasionally be found in small antique or print shops. Since I began to collect these, prices have gone up dramatically, so I do not add to my small collection any more. At present I have eight (mostly large) maps of Bohemia (17th and 18th century) hanging on my walls, as well as twelve views of Prague, ranging from 1493 to the middle of the 19th century. The most valuable of these, the earliest view of Prague altogether, is a large woodcut by Schedel from the Latin edition of the *Nuremberg Chronicle*, an incunable dating from 1493. It is fairly rare. In 1990 I saw one in an antique map dealer's shop on the Graben in Vienna, priced at the equivalent of £500 and I have since seen it, in the catalogue of a leading antiquarian map dealer in London, priced at £3,700. Because on the back of it there is a small woodcut of Jews being burnt at the stake in medieval Germany, I mounted the page between two sheets of glass and made a special frame that allows both sides to be viewed.

In the early seventies I was invited to join the Institute of Linguists which had just set up a division called The Translator's Guild. I submitted to what was then called 'the Fellowship examination' in German and in Czech, passed it and became a Fellow. In 1975 I was elected chairman of The Translators' Guild (a post I held until 1979) and, in the same year, vice-chairman of the Institute of Linguists. I remained vice-chairman until 1980 and from 1982 until 1987 I was a member of the Institute's Council.

Both The Translators Association (which embraced literary translators) and the Institute of Linguists with the Translators' Guild (chiefly non-literary translators and teachers of translation) were members of the recently founded International Federation of Translators (*Fédération Internationale des Traducteurs*, in short FIT), which held (and still holds) its congresses every three years. In my new capacity I therefore attended its congress in Nice in 1974 as a member – but not yet, as at all future congresses, as the leader – of the British delegation. At its next congress, in Montreal in 1977, I was elected a member of the FIT Council and a Vice-President. This marked an intensification of my work for the profession, as distinct from actual translation. The FIT Council met four or five times a year, always at different locations: hotel accommodation was traditionally provided by the national host organization and travel expenses were covered by FIT. This meant that I travelled widely, though mostly in Europe, and met a lot of colleagues from different countries. Naturally, these were not just joy-rides: a good deal of serious business was discussed and I often had to make public speeches.

One such council meeting in the early seventies took place in Moscow. Almost as soon as we were established in our hotel, Pierre-François Caillé, the founder of FIT and its President, called me to his room. He wanted to tell me that he had been informed, secretly, that the Russians had given me my visa only because I was a Vice-President of FIT – they had a dossier on me from my anti-Soviet appearances on BBC Television in 1968. I assured him that, obviously, I would watch my step. I have no doubt at all that on all my visits to the Soviet Union I was under surveillance, but I never felt nervous: I was sure that, while I was there on an official invitation, I would be quite safe. I will have some subsequent experiences in Moscow to relate later.

As a Vice-President of FIT I was several times invited to attend the annual Convention of the ATA, the American Translators' Association – on one occasion even to give the inaugural address. On the way to one such convention, in Albuquerque, New Mexico, I spent a day in New York, sightseeing with a colleague, and went up to the top of one of the World Trade Center towers that were destroyed in the terrorist attack on 11 September 2001.

In 1977, in accordance with BBC practice, I was retired. Owing to the fact that I had, for a long time, been a spare-time translator and had always planned to become a full-time translator after my retirement from the BBC, this was not a traumatic event for me at all. Immediately after my retirement I undertook a lengthy lecture and reading tour in the United States. This came about largely thanks to very generous support from the Goethe Institut. I had received five or six invitations from friends at American universities, but in order to make my trip worthwhile I had approached the Goethe Institut for help in getting me a few more fixtures. And they came up with much more than I expected. They suggested that the Goethe Institut in New York should take me over completely: they would plan and organize a continuous string of talks, including those invitations that I already had. Except for my transatlantic flight they would assume all my domestic travel and accommodation costs, and supply me with a complete detailed itinerary. This worked perfectly. Admittedly, because of the dates involved, this itinerary involved some forward and backward flying, and a fat bunch of domestic flight tickets in the name of 'Professor Ewald Osers'. And people everywhere were enormously hospitable and helpful. My host at Rutgers in New Jersey, for instance, drove me to my next appointment at Moravian College in Bethlehem, Pennsylvania. I was usually paid 200 dollars, but at Cincinnati, where my talk was arranged as the 'Taft Memorial Lecture', they paid me 400 dollars, which was quite a lot then for someone who was not a celebrity. Also at Cincinnati I spoke at Hebrew Union College, 'the bulwark of Reform Judaism', as its Principal told me over (non-kosher) lunch, so reformed and liberal, in fact, that they call their synagogue their chapel and did not insist on my covering my head (or, for that matter, theirs) on entering it, though they had a few skull-caps in a bowl by the door for visitors who might feel uneasy entering the House of God uncovered. I spoke at over a dozen universities – on translation problems in general, on the work of the German Jewish poet Rose Ausländer, which I had published (this at Hebrew Union College), on the East German poet Reiner Kunze, and on the Silesian poet Ondra Lysohorsky, all of these illustrated with examples of their work. I particularly remember the cosy atmosphere of Kalamazoo College, the wonderful surroundings of the University of California, Santa Barbara, where I had a friend on the German department's staff, the University of Texas at Austin which had published a considerable number of my translations in their splendid journal *Dimensions*, the University of Kansas at Lawrence, where a former Monitoring Service colleague was a professor and to where I flew in a tiny Cessna trainer plane with only two passengers in addition to the pilot, and San Diego, where I met a former Monitoring Service typist who had married a monitor, but had since been divorced from him. Probably my most prestigious venue was Harvard University, where I had been invited to give a presentation of Jaroslav Seifert and read some of my translations of his poetry. In the audience was another native of Prague, the future Professor Karen von Kunes. I could hardly believe it, but I was accommodated in the apartment used by Winston Churchill during his visits – an apartment furnished with such obviously valuable antique furniture that I was afraid to sit on the chairs. I had been instructed to eat and drink in the Senior Common Room, and the four or five professors there were perfectly charming and, though I made it clear that I was not an academic, treated me as an equal. I had a lovely time there. I returned to England full of gratitude to the Goethe Institut and with my pockets bulging with money. I honestly do not think that any of my talks was worth the generous hospitality I received plus a honorarium of between 200 and 400 dollars.

A distinguished translator colleague and occasional lecturer, himself an American, had told me that after my lectures the girl students would throw me their room keys and even (like groupies) strip off their knickers and fling them to me on the platform. They may have done that for Dylan Thomas, but they certainly did not do it for me. Clearly I have some work to do on my lecturing skills.

PART FOUR

———

Chapter Ten

Professional Travel and Activities

At the FIT 1977 congress in Montreal, which followed immediately upon my American lecture tour, I allowed myself to be persuaded by a Bulgarian colleague, Elena Nikolova, to learn Bulgarian. The Bulgarians were very anxious to find translators into the major languages, these efforts being strongly backed, also financially, by their government. Elena argued that, as I was a fluent Russian speaker, I would find Bulgarian child's play. This was certainly not the case, but I was keen on languages and during my Russian studies had done quite a lot of Old Church Slavonic (which the Bulgarians to this day insist on calling Old Bulgarian). Within a few months I was invited to a three-week 'symposium of friends of Bulgarian language and literature' – they were very fond of long titles – held on the Black Sea coast near Varna, in the 'Recreational Home of Creative Labour', in plain language a holiday home of the Bulgarian Writers' Union, preceded by a few days in Sofia. They paid for everything, even the flight (by their own airline, Balkan, which flew Soviet-made planes). I enjoyed that enormously. I liked Sofia, and even more the Black Sea coast. (From Sofia we flew to Varna on a Bulgarian internal flight.) The large building, with all rooms facing towards the Black Sea, stood on a steep slope, with a short walk down to a wonderful private beach. Accommodation was rather simple – the shower, for instance, a so-called wet-room, sprayed and swamped the whole bathroom, so that it was wise to do whatever else one had to do there before showering – and I had slept in more comfortable beds. But the food was edible, the wine was excellent and plentiful – as was the rakiya, for which I never developed a taste – and most of the people were interesting. Lessons were on a take-it-or-leave-it basis, and quite a few who knew Bulgarian well already, went down to the beach immediately after breakfast. I was quite conscientious and attended the morning lessons, which were over by about 10.30, leaving ample time for a swim before lunch. And after lunch one went down to the beach again – or, if one wished, one could have a siesta. I was less conscientious about the afternoon classes, which started at 5 pm and were mostly talks (in Bulgarian) by Bulgarian writers and poets. Participants from the West were given single rooms, but Soviet-bloc participants had to share double rooms. Over the next few years I was a regular 'friend of Bulgarian language and literature' and much enjoyed this holiday in the sun. Had I relied solely on those classes, however, I would never have learned the language properly. In between these visits to the Black Sea I studied Bulgarian in the old-fashioned way, from two separate text books, and I made quite good progress. More of this later.

During a visit to Prague the (I think: underrated) Czech poet Jaromír Hořec asked me if I would like to visit Jaroslav Seifert with him – he knew him quite well. Obviously I jumped at the idea. Seifert by then was fairly immobile: he was sitting in a large armchair, his crutches were leaning against the wall behind him. But his mind was lively and youthful, and he clearly kept himself well informed on what was happening in the world. He thanked me for the few translations I had made of his poems and I told him that I wished to translate some of the stuff that had appeared only in samizdat form. He thereupon gave me an annotated samizdat copy of *The Plague Column*, with a personal dedication. I remember that he was greatly amused that a country as traditional and conservative as Britain should have a woman as a prime minister (this was under Margaret Thatcher). I think Hořec and I stayed for about an hour.

The Plague Column: Poems by Jaroslav Seifert appeared in 1979, in London and Boston, beautifully produced, in both hard cover and paperback, with an introduction by Sir Cecil Parrott, who had been a popular British ambassador to Prague and a great friend of the Czechs. He later translated Hašek's *Švejk* and wrote a book on Czech music and an extensive study of the *Liberated Theatre* of Voskovec and Werich. Excerpts from *The Plague Column* appeared in the fashionable *Harpers & Queen* magazine – at that time they still covered literature; they do not do so any longer.

I met Jaroslav Seifert a few more times. Whenever I was in Prague I visited him. To say that we became 'friends' would be presumptuous – but we got on very well with each other. The fact is that I felt very much at home with his late poetry – which was why I had decided to translate him in the first place. If in my youthful and perhaps more 'revolutionary' years I was fascinated by the poetry of Josef Hora and František Halas. Now, in my more advanced years, I felt very much in tune with Seifert's late poetry, with his backward-looking, slightly nostalgic mood, and above all with his love of Prague. Somehow I felt that if I were a Czech poet, that was how I would – or would like to – write.

The setting of my visits was always the same. Seifert was sitting in his comfortable armchair – I never saw him get out of it – and his crutches were leaning against the wall behind him. Sometimes his wife was present, totally silent in the background, and sometimes his daughter Jana, who took part in our conversation. (I also remember once visiting her at her office in one of the lesser buildings of the Valdštejn Palace. And on another occasion Seifert's son drove me back into the city in his car.)

During my visits I was mainly a listener. I let Seifert talk. He was a born raconteur, amusing in his reminiscences. I remember him telling me of his last meeting with Roman Jakobson, about seeing him off at the railway station.

A friend had given me a copy of Švabinský's famous lithograph of Seifert in his younger years. I took this along on one of my visits and got Seifert to autograph it for me. He did so, and dated it – 17. X. 82. I had the picture framed after my return to England and it is still hanging in my study.

Perhaps a word should be said about British reaction to Seifert's Nobel Prize. A few days after the announcement a letter appeared in The Times, signed by Robert Pynsent, the professor of Czech in the University of London, and by two of his followers (or perhaps subordinates). This attacked the decision of the Nobel Prize jury, arguing that Seifert was not a major poet, that he was a writer of kitsch, and that his award was just as much a disgrace as years earlier the shortlisting of Karel Čapek. Pynsent is known by those who know him as an eccentric, and I don't suppose the letter made any waves at all. The next day, or the day after, came a forceful rejoinder from Alan Ross, the highly esteemed editor of *The London Magazine* and the editor of *An Umbrella from Piccadilly*.

In spite of my publication of Seifert, silenced and in disgrace because of his courageous stand at the Second Writers' Congress, the

Communist-controlled Czechoslovak Writers Union continued to invite me to Prague, not only to congresses but also individually: they, too, were eager to cultivate translators into English. They even gave me a number of (admittedly not very grand) medals.

My second volume of Seifert's poetry, *An Umbrella from Piccadilly*, was published in 1983. Like *The Plague Column*, this was a translation of the complete original volume – not a selection from it. Both these volumes were before the Stockholm jury when it awarded to him the 1984 Nobel Prize for Literature. When I visited him after the award – on that occasion I had also been commissioned to interview him – he insisted that my translations had been instrumental in getting him the prize. If he really believed this and was not just being polite, then I think he was wrong. I am convinced he would have got the prize even without my translations. Before we started to record our interview I told him that of his many books the one I liked best was *Světlem oděná*, in my translation *Robed in Light*. When I then, with the tape running, asked him which of his collections he liked best, he said: 'The one you've just named – *Robed in Light*.' Naturally I was very pleased.

As soon as the news of his prize got out I was assailed by publishers anxious to produce more of Seifert's poetry in translation. In the end, Macmillan Publishing Co. of New York and André Deutsch in London jointly commissioned me to bring out a big volume that would present a cross-section of his work. Professor George Gibian of Cornell University was to write a biographical introduction and would also translate some of Seifert's autobiographical stories from his volume *Všecky krásy světa*, [*All the Beauty of the World*]. It was a fine volume; it was republished under Macmillan's own paperback imprint Collier Books in 1990. An enlarged and revised edition – if I may run ahead – was published by Catbird Press in the USA in 1998.

The official Czech reaction to Seifert's Nobel Prize was interesting. The authorities clearly did not know what to do. Here was a writer sidelined for his anti-government attitude receiving the highest international literary award. With so many Czechs listening to foreign broadcasts it would clearly be impossible to hush the matter up completely. Besides, in spite of Seifert's political stance, they inevitably felt flattered that the Nobel Prize for Literature had gone, for the first time ever, to a Czech. The first reports in the press were brief and inconspicuously placed news reports. And one or two volumes of Seifert's poetry – I saw this with my own eyes – appeared in the shop window of the

Czechoslovak Writers' Union bookshop on Národní, with a little card stating that he had received the Nobel Prize.

Circulation and sale, and perhaps even reviewing, of my big Seifert volume (mentioned above) was forbidden in Czechoslovakia. Helena Kocourová, the director of Dilia, the Czechoslovak copyright agency, actually showed me a handwritten note from Miroslav Müller, the Communist Party Central Committee member responsible for culture, describing the book as *závadná*, flawed – clearly because of its reference to Seifert's speech at the Second Congress of the Writers' Union. However, Müller's successor Jaroslav Čejka, whom I knew and whose poetry I had translated, described Müller's ruling as 'nonsense' and in my presence revoked the ban. The book, in its revised and enlarged form, is now in all the major bookshops in Prague. There is no doubt in my mind that I owe most of my Czech honours to my translations of Jaroslav Seifert.

Some time after the publication of my *Umbrella from Piccadilly* there was a 'Piccadilly Festival' with, one afternoon, a reading by me from my translation in a church on Piccadilly.

In the late seventies the members of the FIT Council were invited to a conference on literary translation to be held partly in Moscow and partly in Erevan, Armenia. In Moscow, before a fairly large audience of academics and students, I gave a paper on *Translating Russian Poetry into English*. Those present included the famous Professor Andrey Fedorov, a protagonist of 'poetical translation', if necessary at the expense of fidelity to the text. He challenged some of my arguments, speaking in Russian. The chairman of the conference then turned to me: 'Perhaps Mr. Osers would like to reply to Professor Fedorov?' I asked: '*Svobodno po-angliyski ili s ošibkami po-russki?*' ['Fluently in English or with mistakes in Russian?'] A chorus went up: *Po-russki*! And so I argued my case in Russian. I had much the same discussion at a congress in Vienna some years later: there was then a considerable split between the 'Russian' and the 'Western' schools of poetry translation.

We were then flown to Erevan from Moscow's internal airport of Domodedovo. I have never seen such confusion and chaos at an airport. Even when we had eventually boarded, the locals, probably mostly Armenians, just would not settle down. They moved up and down the aircraft, embracing and greeting friends, before the desperate air hostesses at last managed to calm them. The flight over the snow-capped

Caucasus was wonderful, and Erevan was a beautiful town, with hundreds of fountains in the streets. We were met at the airport by the entire board of the Armenian Writers Union, who made us drink a lot of champagne in a VIP lounge before we even left the airport building. We were taken to the national archives, where the curators explained things to us in excellent English and French, and we were driven to the tomb of Mesrop Mashtots, the fifth-century translator of the Bible into Armenian and the inventor of the Armenian alphabet. For some reason or other – I think because I was the oldest Russian-speaking Westerner in the group – I was asked to make an off-the-cuff speech. We were driven around in a small bus and, somewhere in the mountains, we were given 'lunch' – the longest meal I ever had in my life. It went on for five hours, there were countless (mainly small) courses, and there were nibbles on the table to fill the gaps between courses. There was also some dancing during the meal – I mean: by ourselves, not by a troupe. I think we were all slightly drunk at the end of it, but it was very enjoyable.

The following day, a Sunday, we were taken to Echmiadzin, the spiritual capital of Armenia, and the seat of the Catholicos, the head of the autocephalic Armenian Church. (He is a 'Holiness' and ranks equal with the Pope.) We watched him leave the cathedral in procession and saw the people rush forward to kiss his hand or the hem of his vestments. Our Russian 'minders' were clearly rather discomfited by this show of Armenian loyalty to the Catholicos and hastened to explain that this had nothing to do with religiosity, but that the Catholicos was simply a 'very popular man'. These girls, very pleasant and intelligent girls, did not have an easy time with us Westerners. They had to feed us the official line, they knew perfectly well that we did not believe it, and we knew that they knew that we did not believe it. But we were the guests, we were generously treated and entertained, and we played along.

We were also shown over the Catholicos's palace in Echmiadzin: nothing like the Vatican collections, of course, but a lot of very fine objects all the same.

I had met one of our hosts, Levon Mrktchian, at the FIT congress in Montreal. After that congress, in a book he had written about it, he had called me 'the highlight', mainly because I had received the C.B. Nathhorst Prize there. He suggested that I should translate a collection of 101 'hayrens' of the medieval Armenian poet Nahapet Kuchak: I would have at my disposal not only the poetical translations made by the Russian poet Valeriy Bryusov, but also accurate literal translations, *podstrochniki*, made by himself. It seemed an attractive offer, and Levon whisked me off by car straight away to the Armenian state publishing house, where I signed a contract. Back at the hotel he took me to meet William Saroyan – who normally lived in California, but happened to be on one of his frequent visits to Armenia – who enthusiastically agreed to write an introduction to the book, which of course did not even exist then. But it was eventually published in 1979, as a very pretty book with delightful quasi-medieval ornaments, in the nature of an illuminated manuscript. I was also paid some money, which I deposited in a Moscow Savings Bank account.

Towards the end of the 1970s I was invited to work for the Western European Union's Assembly in Paris. This was an engagement for about a week. The meetings of the Assembly were of course covered by simultaneous interpreters, but for the printed record – a verbatim record like the British Hansard – a more accurate translation was required and that was where our small team of translators came in. It was interesting work, not too difficult for a person familiar with political and current-affairs material, it was well paid, and I enjoyed my brief stay in Paris. I did this for two years running – after which, for economy reasons, the Western European Union decided not to involve translators who had to be brought in from abroad.

In the early 1980s I received an unexpected invitation to MacMasters University in Hamilton, Canada, to a conference on the translation of German poetry. I had never been to that university and I did not know anybody there. It was a prestigious invitation: they paid for my flight, I was one of only half a dozen invited speakers and I was accommodated in the President's lodgings. Other main speakers were Michael Hamburger, Hans Magnus Enzensberger, and Richard Exner. I gave a major (nearly one-hour long) paper on the translation of poetry from German into English; this was later published, more than once, in America and in Europe, and shorter versions and excerpts from this paper served me on several subsequent occasions. In addition to this presentation I also had a totally unscripted and enjoyable platform discussion with Richard Exner, some of whose poetry I had by then translated. We discussed (and sometimes amicably argued) about these translations, and – though I am saying so myself – our audience was most reluctant to let us go, asking for more.

I have often wondered what it was that made a performer, or the work he performed, to hold an audience spellbound. I have given my Seifert 'presentation' four of five times – at Harvard University and at different places in England. It has always gone down very well – how could Seifert's wonderful poetry not go down well? – but only once, while reading at London University's School of Slavonic and East European Studies, did I feel that I was really holding the audience in my hand. There was a breathless silence and you could have heard the proverbial pin drop. I have no idea why this should have been so: I don't think I read the poetry any differently from all other occasions. But it was a gratifying, and possibly a humbling, experience.

About that time I also translated quite a few plays and radio plays. Two of these were broadcast by the BBC – *Détour* (*Objíždka*) by Pavel Landovský and *A Husband for Marcela* (*Ženich pro Marcelu*) by Ivan Klíma. Another Klíma play, *Room for Two* (*Pokoj pro dva*) was being prepared for transmission but was, at the last moment, probably for reasons of economy, cancelled. I also translated two delightful plays by Jiří Mucha, *Dancer in the Dark* – this I translated also into German – and *Fireflies*. The former is about the Latin poet Ovid's banishment (for political reasons) to what today is Romania, but at a deeper level it is about the exile of a creative person generally. I always thought this would be an ideal play for a university dramatic group, but unfortunately, so far, it has not been staged or broadcast. The other play of his that I translated was a very amusing comedy in which fireflies aroused sexual libido in humans.

I don't remember when or how I made the acquaintance of the Czech composer Petr Eben. But I do remember that soon he asked me to translate a few of his songs on poems by František Halas. These were to be 'singing translations'. I remember handing them over to him in the ground-floor café of the Obecní dům in Prague. He was very pleased with them and I suggested that, if he ever wrote an opera – he had in fact been commissioned by the National Theatre to do so – he might consider me for an English translation. So far this has not come about.

About the same time I made the acquaintance of the Czech composer Antonín Tučapský, who lives in London and who has become a frequently performed composer, and of his English wife Beryl, a fine soprano who occasionally gave recitals with her husband accompanying her at the piano. I produced a 'singing translation' of an anti-war choral work of his, but I don't think this has ever been performed in English.

In 1984, to my great delight, I was elected a Fellow of the Royal Society of Literature, the first literary translator to be so honoured, and signed my name in its Fellows' Book with Lord Byron's (by then rather scratchy) pen. Over the years I have attended quite a few of the lectures – not nearly as many as I would have liked and not nearly as many as I would have attended had I been living in London. I am very proud of being a Fellow and also very humble in the face of the many interesting people I have met there. So many of the Fellows are real literary giants, hardly appreciated in a society that attaches greater value to pop group celebrities.

I suppose every translator experiences something unusual or surprising in the course of his or her career. One day I received a letter from an international oil company, inquiring if I would be willing to translate a few articles for a glossy magazine they were publishing for publicity purposes. But there was one condition to my getting the job: I must charge them a very high fee. They must be sure that they had the most expensive translator in the world, and they would make this point – which they said was of importance to their image – in the magazine. I was only too happy to meet their request.

In the eighties, also, I was beginning to receive some foreign honours. In 1980 the BDÜ, the German Translators' Union, made me an honorary member and two years later, in 1982, I received their prestigious Golden Pin of Honour. In 1983 I was given the Silver Pegasus of the Bulgarian Writers' Union. In 1986 I received what was until then my highest decoration, the Gold Medal of the Czechoslovak Society for International Relations. This was presented to me by the then Chargé d'Affaires at the Czechoslovak embassy, Zdeněk Vaníček, who soon became a good friend and who later proposed my name to the Czech parliament for the honour I received in 1997. He is also a very talented painter and poet, and a volume of his poetry, in my translation, was published in England in 1999.

In 1987 I won the European Poetry Translation Prize (the judges that year were Peter Porter and Al Alvarez). From then on there was scarcely a year when I did not receive some prize or honour. Still in 1987, I received the Vítězslav Nezval Medal of the Czech Literary Foundation, as well as the Pierre-François Caillé Medal for services to the translating profession, and, as I shall shortly mention, my Bulgarian order.

It was in the 1980s that the Bulgarians began to reap their rewards for the many seaside holidays they had given me on the Black Sea coast and for other invitations which had enabled me to see Veliko Tărnovo and the Rodope mountains. My first volume of translations from Bulgarian was *The Road to Freedom: Poems by Geo Milev*, published first in Sofia in 1983 and republished in London in 1988. My second volume was *Poems by Nikola Vaptsarov*, the great cult figure of Bulgarian poetry; this was published, both in hard cover and in paperback, in London in 1984. It was followed, in 1986, by *Stolen Fire: Poems by Lyubomir Levchev* and in 1988 by *Fires of the Sunflowers: Poems by Ivan Davidkov*. After the first two of these four volumes of translated Bulgarian poetry I was awarded the Order of Saints Cyril and Methodius (First Class). On that occasion, when I flew out to collect it, the Bulgarians sent me a First Class flight ticket, but on their planes the only difference was that the lunch included a hot meat course that came wrapped in tin foil. The seats were just the same. However, I was met at the airport by a small delegation headed by Lyubomir Levchev, the chairman of the Bulgarian Writers Union. They met me at the foot of the steps off the plane, made me hand my passport and luggage check to one of their underlings, who would go through the formalities for me, and took me to the VIP lounge, where they hosted me with rakiya. The ceremony itself, in the 'Blue salon' of the Writers Union, was attended by several leading writers and poets, including Blaga Dimitrova, a future Vice-President of Bulgaria. Naturally – I knew what was coming and was prepared for it – I made an acceptance speech in Bulgarian. I was one of three *Ordenonostsi* in England, one of the others was Professor Michael Holman of Leeds University, by now retired. We usually met, each wearing our pretty pale-blue ribbons, at the Bulgarian Embassy reception on their *Den na kulturata*.

Quite a few of my translations of Bulgarian poetry also appeared in English-language literary journals inside Bulgaria, so that before long I had quite a bit of money in Sofia. As this money could not be transferred, I decided to buy a Bulgarian carpet, a goat's hair rug. This turned out to be quite an amusing adventure from start to finish. I bought the rug, about 3 by 4 metres in size, at the Sofia TsUM – the equivalent of the Moscow GUM. With some difficulty I carried it to the bedlinen department and, to the delight of the giggling salesgirls, asked for a bed-sheet, a matrimonial-size sheet. They evidently thought I was about to set up house and tried to convince me that I needed at least two sheets. But when I explained to them that I wanted it for wrapping my carpet into it for transport to England, they co-operated cheerfully. Having bought the sheet I wanted to buy some strong string. String, they told me, was not on sale in Bulgaria, but if I followed them to a small room behind the public part of their section, they would, unofficially, let me have as much as I wanted. They unwound metre after metre from a colossal ball of string, all the time asking: '*Stiga?*' – enough? '*Ne stiga*,' I said. I needed more. In the end I had enough. I staggered out into the street with my carpet, sheet and string and fortunately found a taxi to take me to my hotel. There a helpful chambermaid, under my direction, rolled up the rug as tightly as possible, wrapped it in the sheet, and then corded it up rather like those German salamis which are all tied up with string.

That evening Lyubomir Levchev, the chairman of the Bulgarian Writers' Union, gave a dinner for me, prior to my leaving the next morning. I related my experience to them and added, more or less as a joke, that I hoped I would get the thing to the airport in the morning and that I would not be charged excess baggage. Levchev, always a grandee, said: 'We'll take care of that. We'll pay the excess baggage.' Bulgarians are very ready to promise things – and at the time they mean it – but are apt to forget about their promises afterwards. So I did not take Levchev's assurances too seriously. But I was wrong. When I turned up at Sofia airport in the morning, a young man came up to me, said he was from the Writers' Union and was instructed to take care of my carpet. Which he did.

When I arrived at Heathrow I had quite a problem getting the carpet roll and my case on one of the trolleys. Obviously, if only because I was so conspicuous, I went through the red channel. I told the customs officer the whole story – how I had to buy something for the money I could not transfer, and that this was it. I was fortunate: the customs officer was sympathetic. 'But that's most unfair,' he said. 'If they had paid you in hard currency you'd have put it in your pocket and that would have been that.' I had deliberately kept my bill for the carpet. With a wink the customs officer said: 'But you've been shamefully overcharged. We'll base our calculations on what I think the rug is really worth.' So he put down a ridiculously low figure, then consulted his tables and said: 'I'll charge you the lowest permissible rate.' He arrived at an absolutely negligible sum, which I happily paid, and we parted like old friends.

In 1985 I first attended the Struga Poetry Evenings in Macedonia, and I fell in love with the setting immediately. Struga is a lovely little town on Lake Ohrid, not far from the slightly larger Ohrid, and the traditional poetry festival had been going on for many years. Invited participants were very comfortably accommodated at the Hotel Drim, and quite well (if a little monotonously) fed. Immediately in front of the hotel, reached by a short walk through its garden, was a sandy beach, equally popular with the local population and the festival participants. The German and Dutch poetesses – as was then the fashion – went topless, their bare bosoms (perhaps rightly so) attracting more attention than their poetry. The water was definitely on the cool side, but most of us went in and enjoyed a daily swim. Each year there was a full-day excursion by steamer to the ancient monastery of Sveti Naum, which has wonderful frescoes. On the far shore of the lake was Albania.

There were lots of scheduled as well as unscheduled readings and discussion meetings, and attendance used to be very international, with participants even – admittedly not many – from as far afield as America, Australia and Japan. There always is a big platform built on the bridge over the Drim river, where, under glaring floodlights, some 30 foreign poets read a poem each, followed by an (often very bad) translation into Macedonian, read by Macedonian actors. There is a an audience of many hundreds, perhaps thousands, along the two banks of the river, who are able to follow the reading through powerful loudspeakers, and the whole proceedings are also televised and watched, allegedly, by at least a quarter-million viewers. (Very different from reading one's poetry to an audience of maybe forty at the Poetry Society in London or at a poetry festival.) The highlight of the event is the crowning of a famous poet with the Golden Wreath, followed by a ceremony in the ancient Saint Sophia cathedral in Ohrid, when the laureate would read some of his (or her) poetry. I have seen three poets crowned – Yanis Ritzos (1985), Desanka Maksimović (1988), and Ted Hughes (whose unofficial British Council-assisted minder I was, in 1994.) I had been teaching myself a little Macedonian – which is about as close to Bulgarian as Slovak is to Czech – but decided to attend a three-week course run in Ohrid by the University of Skopje in order to learn the language properly. Here, too, accommodation and food were free. But this was not the holiday-camp atmosphere of the Bulgarian 'symposium' on the Black Sea. This was like being back at school. There were three classes: beginners, advanced, and for professional Macedonian scholars. On the first morning I joined the beginners' class, but by lunchtime, because of my knowledge of Bulgarian, was 'kicked upstairs' to the advanced students. The top class was entirely for Austrian, American and Canadian professors of Macedonian, as a kind of refresher course. Our formal lessons were every morning from 9 to 12, with a lecture in Macedonian in the later part of the afternoon. It really was like being back at school: there was a blackboard and we each had exercise books. Unlike Struga, there was no beach near the hotel, but there were two small beaches about twenty minutes' walk away. In the evenings there were optional classes in Macedonian dancing. It was definitely a working holiday, but it was very enjoyable. And I learned quite a bit of the language. Indeed I am probably the only one of those who read their poetry in Struga to have, on my last visit, provided my own translation into Macedonian – although I did have it checked by a native speaker. But my announcement '*Prepev od samiot avtor*' went down very well.

Macedonian uses the same verb for 'playing' and 'dancing'. So when, at one of the Struga poetry events, a young Macedonian woman – who had on her visiting card 'Judge – Poet' – suggested, as I thought, that we should play with each other, it turned out later that she had no more in mind than that we should dance together.

In 1988, having put my new knowledge to good use, I received the Golden Pen of the Macedonian Translators' Union for the first translation of Macedonian poetry published in England. This was followed in 1989 by the Austrian Translation Prize for my translations of several books by Thomas Bernhard.

In the late seventies a small English poetry publisher suggested to me that I might wish them to publish some of my own poetry. I agreed. The slim volume, a collection of 'poetical postcards', was called *Wish You Were Here*. A few years later, in 1995, a more extensive collection – which, however, included most of my poems from the earlier volume – was published under the title *Arrive Where We Started*, a quote from T.S. Eliot.

In 1985 my friend and colleague Zlata Kufnerová decided to translate my poetry into Czech, and a very attractive volume, with line drawings by Ota Janeček, was published by Odeon in Prague in 1986 under the title of *Anamnéza*.

A few years later we thought we might try, together, to produce a Czech selection of Gavin Ewart's poetry. Gavin, whom I knew from meetings of the Royal Society of Literature, was then the best-selling English poet – a position to which Wendy Cope succeeded about ten years later. His humour, a serious humour if there is such a thing, appealed to the British public, and not just to the regular readers of poetry. His public readings, for instance at Waterloo Station, drew enormous crowds. So Zlata and I produced a volume called *My spokojení pozorovatelé zkázy*, published by Odeon in Prague in 1992.

I was by then being increasingly often invited to international conferences to speak on translation problems. I had given dozens of papers in English and a few in Czech, but I had never given one in German. So when I was invited to a conference in Leipzig, where papers had to be given in German, I found it surprisingly difficult to write my contribution on 'Distortion of Language Norms in Poetry and Resulting Translation Problems'. But it went very well and there was a lively discussion afterwards. This Leipzig conference was altogether an interesting experience.

I had never been to the German Democratic Republic before. The surprises began with getting my visa at the GDR embassy in London. The visa department in the basement was like a fortress, with bullet-proof glass between applicant and official, and various security measures. This was not my first visa to a Communist country: I had repeatedly obtained Czech, Soviet, Bulgarian and Yugoslav visas, but at no other embassy had I encountered such an extreme feeling of 'enemy country'. I flew into Berlin-Schönefeld, the airport in the Soviet-controlled part of Berlin. I was met there by a FIT colleague, with whom I got on very well and who had intended to put me up at his home. However, the authorities had forbidden him to do so – the official line being that as a Vice-President of FIT I had to be accommodated in a more luxurious guest apartment on Unter den Linden. I did not mind in the least, but he felt a little embarrassed.

The following day I took the train to Weimar, which I wanted to see – Goethe's town – and where I had arranged to meet Hanns Cibulka, a German poet, though originally from the Czech border region, from Jägerndorf / Krnov, whom I had translated. This worked out very well and we did some sightseeing in Weimar. The train journey was an eye-opener to me. The Czechs, who tend to have an inferiority complex vis-à-vis the Germans, assured me that the GDR, though of course lagging behind West Germany, was economically much more advanced than Czechoslovakia. But this was not my impression at all. The railway stations through which I passed looked as though the war had ended only the week before, and the buildings in Weimar – except for the tourist sights, like Goethe's home and his Garden House – were in an even worse state than those in Prague at the time. The East German state, Cibulka explained to me, did not want to take them over because it lacked the money to restore them, and their private owners, who were receiving rentals pegged down by the government for social reasons, likewise lacked the money. So they were slowly becoming more and more derelict. In Leipzig we visited, as a group, the Thomas-Kirche, the church where J. S. Bach had been the organist and official composer of sacred music, and after the conference were taken to a concert in the re-built Gewandhaus.

One of the honours that gave (and still gives) me the greatest pleasure was the honorary degree – Dr.h.c.phil. – awarded to me in 1990, shortly after the fall of Communism, by the Palacký University in Olomouc. This was a wonderful occasion. The Rector then was Professor Josef Jařáb, later a Senator, an expert on English and American literature. First I had to be fitted out with cap and gown: the Rector's secretary had to raise the hem and shorten my sleeves with pins – evidently I was shorter than most of their doctors. The ceremony began with the National Anthem, after which, headed by the Rector, the Dean and the Promotor, the 'platform party' entered in procession. The Aula was crowded: I expect all the faculty members had been asked to attend. There were speeches, or laudationes, by the Rector and the Dean, and the Latin address by the Promotor. I began my acceptance speech – which of course I had prepared – by expressing my pleasure that I was now receiving the degree which, half a century earlier, Hitler's invasion of Czechoslovakia had prevented me from receiving. I spoke about English-Czech relations and the problems of bringing Czech literature to the anglophone reading public. One of the professors afterwards told me that my speech had been 'more like an inaugural lecture than an acceptance speech'. In addition to the Honorary Doctorate Medal on a red-white-and-blue ribbon – not quite the *catena aurea* of the Promotor's formula – I was, during a drinks ceremony at the Rector's office, also presented with the university's memorial medal. When I was asked to sign the book of honorary doctors I found that there was only one name before my own – Václav Havel.

The following year, 1991, the President of the Federal Republic of Germany, Dr. Weizsäcker, awarded me the *Verdienstkreuz erster Klasse des Verdienstordens der Bundesrepublik Deutschland* – in its official English translation, the Officer's Cross of the Order of Merit of the Federal Republic of Germany – 'for promoting British-German relations by the translation of German literature'. My investiture was a more private ceremony, but attended by family members and some translator colleagues, at the German embassy in London.

In 1992 – by which time my second volume of Macedonian poetry had appeared in England – I received the Joint Prize of the Macedonian Writers' Union and Translators' Union. There were no awards in 1993, but in 1994, after attending the Struga Poetry Evenings and a translation conference in Tetovo, I was given the Macedonian Literature Award.

After the death in 1979 of Pierre-François Caillé, the President of the International Federation of Translators, the socialist countries – this was the height of the Cold War – made a concerted effort to capture the presidency. It must be said openly that quite a few of the leaders of the Western members of FIT did not view such a development with any alarm at all. It was unfortunately only too obvious that the translators' organizations in the so-called capitalist countries, where they enjoyed no financial support from the state, were in no position to compete with the state-funded translators' organizations in the East.

There had been an irregularity at the FIT Congress in Nice in 1974, when the elected Bulgarian member of the Council 'offered' to cede her seat to a colleague, Anna Lilova, the wife of the powerful Alexander Lilov, the second man in the state, immediately after Zhivkov. This was the first congress I attended, as a member of the British delegation. No one objected: it was felt that if the Bulgarians wanted to switch their representative on the Council, there was no harm in it and it might even be of some advantage to FIT to have someone on the Council with a power-base.

In retrospect, now that the Cold War is over, I am finding it difficult to understand why the Socialist countries should have attached quite so much importance to holding key positions in what was, after all, an unpolitical association of translators' and interpreters' organizations with no real power. But prestige evidently meant a great deal to them. Very shortly after Caillé's death the FIT Executive was invited to Sofia and it was agreed that Anna Lilova, as a Vice-President, should hold the presidency on a temporary basis until the next Congress, to be held in Warsaw in 1981, where Council membership would be up for election and the presidency and vice-presidencies filled. I had been Caillé's chosen successor – he told me that, unlike the other possible candidates, I was *un homme de culture* – but the Eastern bloc representatives succeeded in persuading Caillé's widow, who was still too devastated to offer much opposition, to endorse Lilova's provisional appointment. I was, as a kind of consolation prize, made the Director of *Babel*, the quarterly magazine of FIT as well as its representative on the International Book Committee. I did not mind too much because I thought I would probably win the contest in Warsaw.

There had been, over the years, a kind of gentlemen's agreement that each 'side', in order to ensure continuity, would vote for four or five candidates put up by the other side. But in Warsaw, in 1981, this agreement was blatantly broken by the Socialist countries. Late at night the Bulgarians sent an emissary to my hotel room to ask me to withdraw my candidature for the presidency. I declined to do this. So when the vote was counted the following day it turned out that the 'Socialist countries had not voted for anyone on our list, although we had kept to the agreement and voted for their candidates. The result was that I did not even get enough votes to retain my seat on the Council, and Hans Schwarz, in spite of being perhaps the most popular person on the Council, only just scraped in. He was outraged by this breach of a promise: *Sie hat es mir in die Hand versprochen* – she promised and gave me her hand on it, he kept saying.

So the presidency went to Anna Lilova. She must have had a very bad conscience, because she failed to turn up for the traditional party that concluded the Statutory Congress. I do not deny that I was disappointed and hurt, and also angry with myself for having believed that, in the middle of the Cold War, the other side would behave like gentlemen. Members of many delegations sought me out afterwards to express their disgust; a member of the Czechoslovak delegation told me in confidence that they had been threatened with serious consequences on their return home if they did not obey the command that applied to all the Communist delegations. And, to give her credit, the political leader of the Bulgarian delegation, Leda Mileva, an important political figure in her country, came to me after the election to assure me that there was nothing personal in it, but that it was natural that each side should play to win. In point of fact, we became quite good friends and, as I discovered much later, it was she who put my name forward for the Cyril and Methodius Order. I also found out that the FIT representatives of the Socialist countries had frequent 'policy meetings' in Sofia, at which keeping me out of office was a regular item on the agenda. (This was not in any way illegal.) Ironically, I also had some powerful friends in Bulgaria, notably Lyubomir Levchev, the chairman of the Bulgarian

Writers' Union and an opponent of Lilova's husband. In consequence I continued to be invited to Bulgaria,

Did – one is bound to ask thirty years later – FIT benefit from the fact that its President was an Eastern bloc figure? Honesty compels me to admit that the answer is probably yes. No Western translators' organization, unsupported as they all were (and are) by their governments, could have hosted Council and Executive meetings on a similarly generous scale. On more than one occasion, we were actually accommodated in Sofia in the 'government-and-party hotel'. Admittedly, we were not allowed to have breakfast in the hotel in case we overheard the private conversation of Bulgaria's top people; we had to go to a stand-up café nearby for our breakfast. And one of us found that, on turning on the water in his bathroom, it came out of the tap black. But we should not forget that Bulgaria was the poorest country in the Soviet orbit and that, a mere thirty years earlier – I was told this by an eye-witness – the people in Sofia would walk along their (then unsurfaced) streets barefoot, carrying their precious pair of shoes in their hands.

Anyway, after three years 'in the wilderness', during which, as Director of *Babel*, I was entitled to attend Council meetings, I was re-elected to the Council and to a Vice-Presidency at the next Congress, in Vienna in 1984. Amusingly enough – this was not long after the Falklands War – the Argentinian delegate actually voted for me, possibly because, while lobbying for votes, I had addressed her as '*la mas bonita muchacha del Congreso*'. I am not ashamed of this piece of diplomatic flattery: she really was the prettiest girl at the Congress. (And I had by then learned to play to win.) I held these positions in FIT until in 1987, at the age of seventy, I laid down all my public offices. After that I was elected a member of the Council of Elders of FIT and I hold this (purely honorary) function to this day.

In the early eighties our South Korean colleagues, the Korean Society of Translators, generously invited the members of the FIT Council, as well as myself, even though I was not then on the Council, to South Korea for a week, even covering our travelling expenses. In the eyes of the Communists, and perhaps with some justification, South Korea was then, ever since the Korean War and the partitioning of the country, an enemy state and an anti-Soviet American outpost. This meant that the Eastern bloc representatives on the FIT Council did not accept the invitation. The rest of us decided that, as we would be in the Far East at no cost to ourselves, we would add, at our own expense, a week in Japan.

This was organized by our French colleagues. I had never been to the Far East before and it was a wonderful experience. I had to fly from London to Paris, Charles de Gaulle airport, and from there take an airport bus to Paris's other airport, Le Bourget, from where our flight to Seoul would start. Amusingly enough I met several of my colleagues already on the airport bus; they had flown in from Frankfurt, Brussels, Amsterdam, etc., and had boarded the bus at another gate. It was an enjoyable, if lengthy, flight, with a refuelling stop at Anchorage, Alaska. We were flying with the Korean airline, and before serving any meal or drinks the cabin crew changed from their European-style uniforms into traditional and very colourful dress – adding to the unreal, fairy-tale aspect of our trip. After ten or eleven hours we landed at Anchorage. The airport building, or at least the part we were ushered into, was like a huge emporium of luxury goods – expensive furs, objets-d'art carved from walrus ivory, and jewelry. One could also, if one wished, have a special (unofficial) stamp put into one's passport to show one had been in Alaska. The second half of the flight took another eleven hours and somewhere we crossed the international dateline, which made us a day younger, but unfortunately on the way back we gained that day again.

Seoul is a modern American-style big city with very little to remind one that one is in the Far East. But the National Museum with its wonderful collection of ancient Korean art was certainly worth a visit. Which is more than I would say of the Olympic stadium, then still under construction, or the automobile factory and shipyards of Pusang, in the south of the country. But the bus ride through the Korean landscape was beautiful. There is one embarrassing experience I remember. At a reception the Seoul University professor of English literature asked me what I thought of 'Miss Clisty'. I must have looked rather blank, because he added that surely I must have heard of the spectacular success of 'The Mousetlap'. Only then did I realize that he was referring to Agatha Christie. Of course, one knows about the difficulty Koreans, Chinese and Japanese have with distinguishing between R and L – in fact one had known about it ever since, at landing, the loudspeakers in our plane expressed the hope that we had enjoyed our fright – but in actual conversation it takes a while to adjust to it.

Next came Japan. Tokyo I did not find interesting: a huge swarming American city with Japanese letters everywhere. Except that, unlike America or Europe, there are pretty young ladies in kimonos in all the major stores, whose sole duty it is to bow to customers as they step onto or off the escalators. Another thing I liked was that, for the benefit of foreigners who could not read a Japanese menu, there were coloured papier-maché representations of the different dishes, so that you only had to point to the one that tempted you. At least they had chairs in the Tokyo restaurants. In the smaller places in rural Japan we were made to sit on the floor, or actually on very thin mats, having taken our shoes off on entering. Some of us soon discovered that if you had to sit on the floor with crossed legs, this was much easier if you could lean your back against a wall. I did not find chopsticks easy to handle, but could just about manage if sitting on a chair. Sitting on the floor and using chopsticks was a little too much, and there were occasions when I asked for a spoon.

From Tokyo we went to Kyoto, the ancient imperial capital, by the famous super-fast 'bullet train'. At one point, given the right weather conditions, one could – according to the guidebooks – see Mount Fuji, but I did not. Kyoto was a different world from Tokyo: beautiful temples, tranquil Zen gardens, brilliantly coloured carp in the temple pools. And our Japanese hosts were very hospitable and attentive. (The Japanese translators' organizations are among the wealthiest in the Federation.) We flew back from Osaka to Paris and I continued my flight to London. Nowadays every other person you meet has been several times to Hongkong, Taiwan, China, Japan, Malaysia, and Thailand – but then, twenty-odd years ago, we felt very adventurous.

My only other visit to Asia, a few years later, was after a translation conference in Moscow. Each of us foreign participants was, after its conclusion, offered the choice of a number of trips – Leningrad, Kiev, Riga, Volgograd (the former Stalingrad) or Tashkent and Samarkand. Needless to say, I chose Tashkent and Samarkand. I had not been to Leningrad, but I felt it would be easy to go there at any time. Unfortunately this opportunity did not arise, and I doubt if it will now. But Samarkand seemed to me the obvious choice – perhaps also because I liked James Elroy Flecker. So we were first flown to Tashkent. At the airport we were loaded into a small bus and with a police car in front of us, flashing its lights and soundings its sirens, we were driven at top speed through Tashkent – I distinctly remember that we 'ran' several red lights – to a 'government guest house'. (Tashkent, of course, was the capital of the Uzbek Socialist Soviet Republic.) The 'guest house' was inside a fenced plot, with a submachine-gun-armed sentry at the gate. It was not only comfortable, but, to the amazement of our Moscow minders, there were dishes piled high with fresh fruit on the dining table – fruit they said they had not seen in years. After supper some of us decided to walk into the town for a little sightseeing; I remember clearly that we made a point of chatting a little to the armed guard at the gate, in the hope that (provided he was not relieved in the meantime) he would recognize us when we returned and let us in. There was no problem. The following day there was a reception at the Uzbek Writers' Union and, because once again I was the oldest, I was made to sit on the platform with our hosts and, moreover, make a speech (in Russian, of course, not in Uzbek) on behalf of all the foreign visitors.

The drive from Tashkent to Samarkand was unforgettable. Our bus was again preceded by an outrider police car – not sounding its siren this time but only flashing its lights. As we reached an Oblast [District] boundary, our bus was handed over to another police car, which had been waiting there for us, our original escort returning to Tashkent. All around us were cotton fields.

Samarkand is a dream – in the sense that Venice is a dream. Over a hundred years ago, in 1888, Lord Curzon, the British Viceroy of India, described the Registan as 'the noblest public square in the world. I know nothing in the East approaching it in massive simplicity and grandeur, and nothing in Europe, save perhaps on a humbler scale the Piazza di San Marco in Venice.' Its main building, the Madrasah of Ulugh Beg, dates from the early fifteenth century, and the other two madrasahs flanking it were built in the seventeenth century, but in close imitation of the original building, so that they form a large harmonious complex of light and dark blue tiles, richly decorated in gold. There are other wonders to see in Samarkand – the mausoleum of Timur, the Tamburlane the Great of Christopher Marlowe, Ulugh Beg's astronomical observatory, and a few mosques. The last evening a German colleague, Ilse Tschörtner, the German translator of Marina Tsvetaeva's poetry, suggested that we share a bottle of Soviet champagne (which she had bought) looking at the Registan in the moonlight. So we sat there, silent with admiration, passing the bottle (as we had no glasses) from mouth to mouth – all with great propriety. Some time later she sent me her Tsvetaeva translations, which were very good, and in the mid-nineties, after the fall of the Wall, when I was in Berlin for a translation conference, she showed me the sights of Potsdam.

We had hoped that we would also be taken to Bukhara and Khiva, reputed to be every bit as beautiful as Samarkand but less touristy – but we were told that these two oases were undergoing repairs to their ancient monuments and were temporarily closed to visitors. Confidentially it was hinted to us that the real reason was that they served as Soviet air bases against Afghanistan – it was the time of the Soviet-Afghan war, possibly the only war the Red Army ever lost.

We flew back to Moscow in a two-tier aircraft – not just an upper deck over the front part as in the Boeing 747, but along the whole length. From the air we could see what we had been told by our Uzbek colleagues – that, as a result of the cotton monoculture ordered by Stalin, and the irrigation necessary for it, the level of the Aral Sea had dropped to such an extent that it was now bisected by a sandbar into two halves. It was extremely doubtful, we were told, that the process would prove reversible.

In the eighties a very well established and prosperous German school network, the *euro-schulen* organization, approached me and a few of my colleagues in the FIT leadership with the invitation to join its *Kuratorium* or supervisory board. This would involve no duties whatever, they merely wanted the names of top figures in the translation world to be on their publicity material. The organization had dozens of schools in Germany and one or two abroad. They ran specialized courses, leading to specialized degrees, all of them involving one or two foreign languages – e.g. Euro-Secretary, Euro-Economist, etc. In many of the *Länder* of the Federal Republic these were officially recognized as professional qualifications. Once a year we therefore flew to Germany, at the expense of the organization, were put up in luxury hotels and taken to meals in luxury restaurants. All we had to undergo was being shown round their establishments – each year in a different location – and listening to a report on the school's activities during the past year. Even after I resigned at age seventy, they very generously sent me presents on my birthday and at Christmas.

At the risk of upsetting the chronology this may be the moment to speak of my last – I mean: most recent, but it probably is my last – visit to Moscow. This was during the second year of Gorbachev and there were a few (rather minor) signs of perestroyka. In a Moscow park we saw a group of (presumably) students with a poster calling on the city administration to do something or other. Not the stuff of revolution, perhaps, but a couple of years earlier the militia would have confiscated the poster and possibly arrested the youngsters. I felt that the political situation was sufficiently relaxed for me to seek out some young poets to collect new work from them with a view to translating and publishing it in England. I also visited the famous Bella Akhmadullina, who gave me the typescript of her latest book – she no longer had any copies of it.

Perestroyka or not, we still each had our minder accompanying us. Officially these young ladies were our 'interpreters', but as this was a conference of translators of Russian literature who all spoke Russian, the 'interpreters' role was hard to justify. But of course it was useful to have a person with local knowledge attending to you, and my minder, Tanya, was a very pleasant and well educated young lady. On one occasion she asked me a 'big favour'. The woman who normally met her little girl from school and took her home was unable to do so – would I therefore mind making my own way back to the hotel? I said: No problem. (Besides, the Ukraina hotel, one of the seven Stalin-Gothic skyscrapers, was visible from nearly everywhere in the city.) Obviously I got back safely. When Tanya collected me the next morning she had evidently been crying. She had got into terrible trouble, she told me, for leaving me alone in the street. I might have lost my way, there could have been an international incident. I tried to put her mind at rest. (A few years later, with travelling becoming easier for Soviet citizens, she came to London and got in touch with me. I said I would take her out to lunch. Over lunch she said she had a confession to make. When she had left me in the street in Moscow, she had got into trouble not because I might have lost my way, but because I might have returned to my hotel room before the KGB had finished searching it.)

Turning a vast country around, from a closed police-state to a more open society, was an enormous task and it would be unreasonable and unfair to blame Gorbachev for glasnost being still very patchy at that time. Thus we foreign delegates were given private showings of two new Soviet films. One of them was *Pokayanie* [*Repentance*], the first public admission of the existence of the gulags, the Siberian penal camps, where millions of political prisoners perished. The film did not in fact show these camps, but it showed, very movingly, logs cut by the camp inmates and floated down the river – with names and personal messages scratched into them. Our hosts clearly wished to convince us that things were changing, that formerly taboo subjects could now be spoken about – but it was not until 1986 that this film was released for the general Soviet public. Even so, it was a first step.

During the latter part of my stay, when I was collecting perestroyka poetry, I had a different minder, whose name I have forgotten. It was she who took me to Bella Akhmadullina's apartment. Upon leaving Moscow, at Vnukovo airport, all my conference colleagues passed through the controls smoothly; only my case had to be opened. Clearly my minder had reported my movements to her superior. 'Export of unpublished material is not permitted,' the official told me. He confiscated it all. 'I hope that perestroyka will reach you, too, one day,' I said to him in Russian. Without batting an eyelid he replied unsmilingly: 'We hope so too.' This incident also had a sequel. A year later Akhmadullina visited England and, as it happened, stayed with a friend quite near where I live. I should come round straight away. And she handed me the material that had been confiscated from me at the airport – or most of it. The airport official had returned it to the Soviet Writers' Union who had handed it to Akhmadullina when they knew she was going to visit England. Was the official at the airport sympathetic to my efforts or was he simply a bureaucrat? I will never know.

On that visit also – foreigners were by then permitted to shop in ordinary shops and not only, as in the past, in the special foreign currency Berezka shops – I decided to 'invest' some of my roubles in a few amber necklaces and bracelets. For the benefit of readers who have never done any shopping in Russia I should explain the procedure. You first chose what you wanted to buy and asked the price. You then went to the cash desk – queuing for a second time – paid and got a receipt. With this receipt you queued once more and eventually exchanged your receipt for your purchase. Our Russian hosts and minders regarded this as a perfectly normal procedure – but surely it was based on the presumption that if a customer received his goods before payment, he would try to run away with them without paying.

Another oddity of shopping in Russia was that the cash register had evidently not yet reached the Soviet Union. Everywhere they were using the abacus. Often very quickly and efficiently – but even so, this was the nation which was then leading in space research, the nation with some of the leading mathematicians in the world.

In the early nineties, while we were wintering in Florida, I had a telephone call from Lord Weidenfeld. Would I be interested in translating the history of the Oppenheim Bank in Cologne. This would be published by Weidenfeld, but as a private, non-commercial publication, to be given away by the Oppenheim Bank to its friends. And the whole thing would be financed by the bank, so I should ask for a generous fee.

They would want the English version to be published in 1995, to mark the 200th anniversary of the bank's foundation. He sent me the German book, which had already been published. I found it quite fascinating: it was not only the history of a private bank, but also a social history of Jewish business in the Rhineland about the time of the French Revolution and the industrial development of modern Germany. I was invited by Baron von Oppenheim to visit the bank in Cologne. We liked each other and I accepted the commission.

The publication of the book, under the title of *Striking the Balance*, in 1995 was a glittering event at Spencer House in London, the former town house of the Earls Spencer (Princess Diana's family), which had only recently been restored to all its former glory. It now belongs to Lord Rothschild. There were a large number of prominent guests and I wore a hired dinner jacket with the ribbons of some of my decorations. As I was talking to Baron Oppenheim and another gentleman, Lady Thatcher appeared in the door, making for our little group. I discreetly withdrew so as not to intrude, but she had observed my manoeuvre and turned to me with outstretched hand: 'No, no, please join us. I am Margaret Thatcher.' Much as I hate her politics, I have to admit that she was perfectly charming. Baron Oppenheim explained that I was the translator of the book (piles of which were standing on each little table) and she questioned me about it with the (no doubt feigned) interest of the professional politician. She was no longer in office at that time.

At the FIT Congress in Brighton in 1993 I chaired and moderated a platform discussion between, first, David Lodge and his French and Italian translators and, next, between V.S. Naipaul and two of his translators. I was astonished then, and still am, at the scant interest these outstanding writers were showing in the quality of the translation of their books into other languages. At an evening event at the same congress, a reading of original and translated poetry, I was introduced – I think: with too fulsome compliments – by Christopher Fry. One of the other readers that evening was Wendy Cope. This event was televised.

In 1995 the Austrian Society of Literature invited me to stay some time in Vienna as its guest – chiefly, I think, because I had received the Austrian Translation Prize for my Thomas Bernhard translations. I could have stayed for two months, but felt that three weeks was the most that I could reasonably leave Mary on her own. I had had an open invitation from the University of Salzburg for some time, so I arranged to spend a few days and give a couple of lectures there. I enjoyed the generous hospitality of the professor of English and American studies, James Hogg. During the two weekends I rented a car and, with a different companion each time, visited some of my childhood holiday venues in the Salzkammergut and in Carinthia. During my final week in Vienna Edith happened to be there as well, en route to friends in Carinthia, and we went together to the Theater in der Josefstadt to see a play by Hofmannsthal and to the Burgtheater to see *Romeo and Juliet* in the translation by Erich Fried, who (recently deceased) had been a friend of mine.

A very large number of poems translated by me had, over the years, been appearing in literary periodicals and anthologies in the UK, in America, and occasionally in Australia. On rare occasions I had submitted these myself – though only unpublished ones – but mostly these had been selected by the editors of these publications from my published volumes of translated poetry. To my own amazement – Mary has been keeping a card index of my published poetry – the total of these publications has by now reached some 1,800. More amusingly, one of my translations, a poem called *Confusion* by the Bulgarian poet Nino Nikolov, was recently chosen for the Poetry in Motion programme operated by the American Poetry Society. I was not even aware of the existence of this scheme, when I was informed of it. These 'poem posters' are displayed in every carriage of the New York Subway and in every bus of the Metropolitan Transit system for a period of three months, and are read – so the American Poetry Society claims – by two million New Yorkers every day. No payment, unfortunately, but the publicity is pleasing: my name as the translator is, of course, on the poster.

In November 2001 the poem poster eventually appeared and I received several copies of it, along with a letter from the Marketing Services Manager of New York City Transit, informing me that there had been an excellent response to the poem, with quite a few inquiries on where the poster might be purchased, and requesting my permission (which of course I gave) to have copies of it put on sale (at $ 4 each) in the New York Transit Museum gift shop. After New York it will go to Portland, Oregon, and eventually to (at least) five other major cities in the USA. (On 13 November 2001 I was informed that the poem posters were up and that – amazingly – a total stranger had spoken about that

poem to the girl friend of the organizer of the programme, who happened to be travelling by Subway.)

In the eighties I was beginning to be increasingly invited to literary and
poetry festivals. One of the earliest of these was the Cambridge festival
in 1983, where I first met Miroslav Holub in person, though I had been
translating his poetry for some time. We read together – he read his
Czech originals and I my English versions. In the interval the BBC man
who recorded the performance sought us out and said: 'Gentlemen, you
two got the most applause. Would you mind very much if we cut some
of it off and stuck it on to the readings of others?' Of course we had no
objections. We read many more times together – the last time in London
in 1997, in the Old Operating Theatre of the South London Hospital.
This is now a museum of the history of surgery, with a collection of ter-
rifying iron instruments – not nickel or chrome. In the small operating
theatre on the second floor we both sat on the operating table, with our
audience sitting on the steeply raked semicircular benches from which
the medical students one hundred and fifty years ago would have
watched the surgeons at their work. Miroslav was in his element: he
knew what all those instruments were for, he joked about them, and the
reading, like all his readings, was hilarious and a great success.

At one festival, in Coventry, where I was invited to speak on the translation of poetry, I was still sitting in the 'artists' room' when I was told I
had a visitor. And to my great astonishment he was the newly appointed
Slovak ambassador to London, Ján Vilikovský, himself a translator and
translation scholar, who had driven there (in his official car) along with
his cultural attaché – a trip of about two hours. I had met him once or
twice before, at translation conferences, but we were not exactly close
friends. I was all the more flattered. In the discussion which followed he
made a point of speaking about my Seifert translations and about what
I had done for Czech poetry. At a time when the 'divorce' between
Czechs and Slovaks had only just taken place I regarded this as a fine
'federalist' gesture. A few years later, when he was no longer in the diplomatic service, he invited me to two 'private' literary conferences in
Slovakia – at Trenčianské Teplice and at Budmerice. (I met him most
recently at a conference in Prague, in the spring of 2001, and we had
lunch together.)

On one occasion the British-East European Council invited the young
Bulgarian woman poet Mirela Ivanova to England and asked me – all

expenses paid – to act as her minder or chaperone (she spoke no English) during some of her stay. She had been invited to read at the Cheltenham Literature Festival, subsequently at Keeble College, Oxford, and later in Leeds. I drove her from London to Cheltenham, read with her at the festival (I had translated some of her work before), drove her back to Oxford, where we had a joint reading with Fleur Adcock and the Romanian poet Nina Cassian, and delivered her to the train for Leeds, where Professor Michael Holman – like myself a holder of the Bulgarian Cyril and Methodius Order – was going to take her over.

In the meantime our children were growing up. Margaret got a place at Sheffield University to study political science and economy – then a fashionable subject – and after graduating with a BSc (Econ) decided to take a one-year's course for career advisors. After gaining her diploma she worked for the public authority as a career advisor for school leavers. In 1971 she got married: our son-in-law Tony Clewett, a graduate of Keele University, was then teaching statistical mathematics at the University of Birmingham and, at the same time, had started a computer business, specializing in statistical software. After some time he gave up his university post to devote himself fully to his business. They have two sons, Martin and David, born in 1975 and 1978. They are both adults now, of course, Martin having taken his degree in physics at Oxford and David a degree in Music and Media Studies at the University of Mid-Lancashire in Preston.

Our son Richard had started to study art history at the University of East Anglia in Norwich, but after a year had dropped out (or been dropped out) when he failed to pass his exam in philosophy, a subject he disliked. He had gone into business, working first in periodical publishing firms and later in computer firms, as a fairly successful sales representative, but when, as a result of Thatchcrite economics, these firms folded up under him, he decided to retrain as a teacher of English as a Foreign Language. He went to the Czech Republic, teaching first at a school at Šilheřovice near Ostrava, then at Rožnov pod Radhoštem. In 1999 he married a Czech (or, more accurately, Moravian) girl, Hana, and now runs his own small English language school in Vsetín in Moravia. He did not know a single word of Czech when he went out there, but is now quite fluent.

As one establishes a name as a literary translator one tends to be invited to join committees and sit on juries. I have never refused such invitations: I remember too well how, as a beginner, I was supported and helped by more experienced members of the profession and I wished to help others in return. For something like seven years I was therefore a member of the Translation Advisory Panel of the Arts Council of Great Britain (now, following some decentralization, the Arts Council of England). The Arts Council, prior to the establishment of our National Lottery, was the principal agency that dispensed Government money for a variety of cultural purposes – from financing the Royal Opera House, funding foreign tours by the principal British orchestras, keeping struggling literary journals alive, to subsidizing the publication of translated literature. This was the task of the committee, or 'panel', of which I was a member. In addition to members of the Literature Department of the Arts Council it included one or two literary academics, a publisher, and one or two translators. Publishers wishing to publish a translated title that did not seem to them to be financially viable, applied to the panel for a subsidy. This was granted provided the panel thought the title deserving of financial help and providing the applicant's contract with the translator was fair and generous. We met about every two months, and it was interesting work. Once or twice – I was sent out of the room on those occasions – a publisher (unbeknown to me) had applied for a subsidy to publish one of my translations, usually of poetry.

For many years the *Independent* newspaper, in a praiseworthy effort to bring more foreign literature to the English reader, established an annual Translated Fiction Prize, consisting generously (for English conditions) of £5,000 for the author of the book and £5,000 for the translator. I was on that jury for a number of years, by far the least famous of its members, who included some of Britain's most distinguished writers – such as A.S. Byatt, Doris Lessing, and George Steiner. We would meet several times a year, compare our opinions of the books entered for the competition and eventually arrive at an agreed decision.

In 1999 I was invited by the Poetry Society to be one of the two judges for that year's European Poetry Translation Prize. My fellow judge was the Irish poet and Oxford don Bernard O'Donoghue. Surprisingly we found ourselves very much in agreement in our assessments of the rather large number of entries – which all needed careful and conscientious reading – and we got on well together.

Now and again in the course of my professional career I was approached with offers for jobs I had never done before. In the mid-

1990s a small opera company in England commissioned me to translate the libretto of an opera by a young Slovak composer, Juraj Beneš. The original text consisted of a series of poems by Janko Král'. My job was not only to translate these folksong-like poems into rhymed English verse, but also to provide a 'singing translation', with stresses and vowels in the right places. I worked from a score of the opera – which was called *Zkamenený* [*Turned to Stone*]. The opera was performed twice, but unfortunately at a time when I was out of the country, so I could not be present at my own opera-stage début. The opera company, Mecklenburg Opera, were so pleased that they got me to translate another opera by a Slovak composer, a fairy-tale opera – but before the job was finished the composer decided to withdraw it for a complete revision.

Another new venture for me was being asked to become one of the team of 'compilers' for the *Oxford Duden German-English Dictionary*. I was only one of a team of maybe thirty, half of them in England and half in Germany. It was an entirely new departure for me, but I found it interesting and enjoyable. Not many days pass without my looking something up in 'my' dictionary.

In 1978 Mary (who had not been to America before) and I decided to try a camping holiday in the States. Our friends in Philadelphia rented a motor home for us from a rental firm near them. An American motor home is rather grander than a European motor caravan. It is, in size and shape, not unlike an ambulance – ours, a small one by American standards, was 21 feet, or about 6.5 metres, long, and a good deal wider than an ordinary car. It could be readily connected to the utilities provided at most American campgrounds – electricity, water, and sewerage. Its 'dinette', two seats with a table between them, converted into a bed, and another bed was in the 'overcab', above the driver's and passenger's seats. It had a shower room with a WC, a kitchenette complete with a double sink, a three-burner gas cooker and an oven, and a fridge/freezer. It also had a warm-air heater and an air conditioner. It was a heavy vehicle and I never really enjoyed driving it in town traffic – but on the wide American roads there was no problem.

On our first motor home trip we decided to travel the Blue Ridge Parkway, a wonderful scenic highway through the Appalachian Mountains to the Cherokee National Forest. One advantage of this 'panoramic' road was that commercial vehicles, i.e., large trucks, were banned from it. We went as far as the Smoky Mountains, saw a Cherokee village – very much stage-managed for visitors, we felt – and then left the mountains and made for New Bern, North Carolina, to visit Tryon Palace, the residence some two hundred years previously, from 1770, of William Tryon, an ancestor of Mary's, who was then the colonial governor of North Carolina. Mary had written to the curator before, so we were received right royally. We enjoyed our motor home experience so much that we decided to spend the following winter in a motor home in America.

Mainly because of Mary's MS and in order to avoid the English winter, we had been experimenting with Majorca and with Tenerife, but we did not find these places really warm enough in midwinter. So we decided to give South Florida a try. I went to the Commercial Department of the American embassy in London, asked for the Yellow Pages of Miami and copied out the addresses of three motor home rental firms. I wrote to all three of them; only two replied, and one of these looked more attractive than the other. And they sounded keen: they offered to collect us from our hotel and drive us to their depot. This worked very well. We had a brief instruction and we were off. I had done a little homework and we had come to the conclusion that we should get away from the Atlantic coast of Florida and make for the Gulf coast. We explored a number of campgrounds in southwest Florida, but even then we liked one near Naples best. After a month there we returned our motor home and – we had planned this in advance – flew out to Los Angeles and hired another motor home there. With this we drove into 'the desert', the Palm Springs and Indio area, and found it exceedingly interesting. But on balance we felt that California was needlessly far away and that Florida would be a better choice. Thus we became 'regular seasonals' at the KOA campground near East Naples, and we spent a four-months winter holiday there for twenty-three seasons.

I was by then retired and, more or less, master of my own time. So we decided to explore some of America during the summer. We flew to Denver, Colorado, rented a motor home there, and drove across the 'Continental Divide', the American Rocky Mountains, the highest point on our route, Fall River Pass, being 3,593 metres. I had skied at altitudes of 3,800 metres, but had never been so high driving a vehicle. We descended into Utah, a scenically wonderful state, and saw several of the canyons – Arches National Park, Bryce Canyon, Zion Canyon – and drove on into Arizona to view the Grand Canyon, moreover from both its rims. Grand Canyon is stunning because of its dimensions, but the most beautiful of the lot is Bryce Canyon with its coral-red rock formations. We returned via New Mexico, where we visited the widow of a cousin of mine in Santa Fè. We liked Santa Fè a lot, with its adobe buildings and its wonderful museum of American native art. We also saw some pueblo villages. We returned to Denver, handed in our motor home and flew back to England.

Except that there was a hitch. We had intended to fly to Philadelphia, stay a day with our friends and then fly on to England. If you are an experienced flyer you can tell by the engine noise if the plane is losing height. And it seemed to me, long before we were due to land at Philadelphia, that we were losing height. After a while the captain's voice came over the loudspeakers: 'We have been instructed by our airline to make a landing at Chicago. When we have touched down, please leave all your luggage on board and exit the aircraft as quickly as you can.' This sounded rather alarming. But a short while later they changed the instructions: we should take our hand luggage with us. I had a window seat. And as we made our final approach I could see fire engines and ambulances lined up along the runway with their strobe lights flashing. We touched down a long way from the terminal building and were bused there. Only when we had all been herded into a gate lounge were we told, with apologies from the airline, that they had received a warning that there was a bomb on board. We would all be put on another aircraft and flown on to Philadelphia shortly. We never discovered – airlines are very cagey about these things – if a bomb or a suspect package had really been found, or whether it was all a hoax.

Instead of hiring a motor home every year we soon bought a second-hand one from friends. And now that we had our own house-on-wheels we decided to explore America during the summer. We therefore cut our hibernation in southwest Florida short and, in early 1984, allowed about a month to drive the roughly 2,500 miles [4,000 km] to Phoenix, Arizona. On the way we did some sightseeing in New Orleans and met up in San Antonio with Professor Leslie Willson of the University of Texas at Austin, who, a few years earlier, had been my host, not just for a lecture at Austin but also putting me up at his home. From El Paso on the Rio Grande, the border between the USA and Mexico, we drove over the bridge into Ciudad Juárez, just so that we could say we had been in Mexico.

We were by then members of the Family Motor Coach Association and had written to the chairman of its 'Arizona Chapter' to inquire if he could recommend some motor home firm in Phoenix, where we could leave our vehicle. Instead he wrote back to say that one of his members, on the edge of the desert not far from Phoenix, would be glad to keep our motor home. So we drove to the address and found the couple exceedingly hospitable, even more so when the husband told me that he came originally from Croatia and I spoke to him in my broken Serbo-Croat. (When we picked up our motor home from him a few months later, he had not only serviced it but, throughout the summer had placed buckets of water in it to prevent wood shrinkage in the Arizona heat and had started up the engine several times to keep the battery in good shape.) After taking over our vehicle he insisted on driving us, with our luggage, back into Phoenix to a hotel he recommended, for our flight home the following day.

After collecting our vehicle some time in the summer we drove west into California and then north, visiting the Sequoia National Park with its incredible nearly three-thousand-year old giant redwoods and the beautiful Yosemite National Park, and on to San Francisco. We followed the coast all the way through Oregon, where unfortunately sea mist prevented us from seeing the spectacular coastline, and through Washington state, avoiding Seattle, which was a good idea, and Vancouver, which was probably a less good idea. In British Columbia, Canada, we followed the Fraser River up into the Canadian Rockies, to Jasper (where deer roamed through our campsite) and down the spectacular Icefield Parkway to Banff. We continued through Calgary and re-entered the United States, making for Great Falls in Montana, and then drove east for one day after another, circumnavigating Chicago, visiting friends on Lake Erie, and stopping at Niagara Falls. Then we went on to Philadelphia, where we left our motor home with our friends, to be picked up again in the autumn and driven down to our winter location in southwest Florida.

In the summer of 1986 we thought we would drive up the Eastern seaboard of the United States, to Vermont and Maine, and then explore Canada's Maritime Provinces. But this time we were unlucky with the weather. When we got to Florida to collect our motor home, the temperature was 104 degrees Fahrenheit, which is 40 Celsius. It was so hot and humid we decided not even to tidy up our vehicle, but drove off straight away, heading north. But in Georgia, 600 miles [1000 km] further north, it was still 104 Fahrenheit, and it was not until we were in North Carolina that the temperature became bearable. We kept driving north and had good weather in Vermont. But as we approached Maine the weather broke: it rained heavily and the forecast for the following week also spoke of heavy rain. So we consulted our camping guide and found a site in Watertown, in upper New York state, which had an indoor swimming pool. There we stayed quite happily for over a week, with excursions to the St.Lawrence river and, across it, into Canada. While we were staying there Lubor Zink – whose garage I had helped build several decades previously – visited us from Ottawa. (His wife, who had once been Czechoslovak Junior Tennis Champion and had played at Wimbledon, was then visiting their son in New Zealand.)

In the mid-1990s we decided that our touring days were over and that we would in future lead a more stationary existence in Florida. We therefore drove to a 'recreational vehicle' dealer and exchanged our motor home for a trailer and – since this could not move on its own – a car. The trailer was nearly half as long again as the motor home, its outside measurements were 31 feet (or 9.5 metres). It had a bedroom, which could even be closed off from the rest of the trailer, and the main advantage was that we did not, as in the motor home, have to convert our seating facilities into beds in the evening and back into seats in the morning. At the other end of the trailer was our 'sitting room' with kitchen, and there was a shower room plus WC. The trailer was solidly anchored down at its four corners, supposedly hurricane-proof. It had electric, water and sewer connection, as well as a telephone at each end and a cable-TV connection with a large number of (mostly unappealing) programme channels. I moreover installed a modem connection into our telephone line, so that I was in e-mail and internet contact with the outside world. Naturally, I took my laptop with me to Florida, and I had a small but very efficient inkjet printer there which I used to leave, over the hot and humid summer, in the air-conditioned office of the campground manager. Our car had a cover tied down over it, but I had an arrangement with a nearby car repair place for it to be collected every year a week before our arrival and given a general service and testing. Certainly life had become a great deal more comfortable.

Chapter Eleven

'I grow old, I grow old
I shall wear the bottom of my trousers rolled...'

(T.S. Eliot)

The only year we missed hibernating in Florida was the winter of 1996/97, when, in November 1996, I had a heart attack and in January 1997 had a quadruple bypass operation. This was very bad timing on my part, because we had hoped to have a real family holiday in Florida that year – with our daughter (with husband and two sons) coming out from Birmingham, our son from the Czech Republic, Mary's sister from Maidenhead, and her son, daughter-in-law and grand-daughter from Basingstoke. Everything had been planned in minute detail, including the taxis ordered to collect them from the Southwest Florida International Airport at Fort Myers – so in the end, as it was too late to make changes, Margaret and her family and Mary's sister with her family went out, without us being there, and thanks largely to the hospitality of our friends there had a wonderful time. Our son Richard instead decided to come over to England to spend Christmas with us, bringing his girl friend Hana with him.

My heart attack, by the 'law of contrariness', occurred at 6 a.m. on a Sunday morning. I realized what it was and got Mary to phone the duty doctor. He came very quickly and immediately ordered an ambulance. I did not feel bad at all and remember joking with the paramedics and asking them why they did not sound their siren. They said, very reasonably, that early on a Sunday morning, with no traffic about, there was no need to. At the hospital in Reading I found myself, at the 'morning round', in the care of the cardiologist whom I had, for a number of years, been seeing once a year as a private patient. The food was pretty awful, but I was looked after well and the nurses were pleasant and cheerful. After about a week I was discharged into the care of my regular doctor and the member of the practice who specialized in cardiac cases. In January it was felt that my heart was not working properly and

I was returned to the hospital for an angioscopy. This revealed that two of my arteries were completely blocked and the third was narrowed down. I was told that, if I wanted to live for more than another year or a year and a half, I had to have a bypass operation. As I had private health insurance this operation could be done in London, at the Harley Street Clinic. I went up to London to meet the surgeon who was going to do the operation and I felt reassured about his competence, just as (or so he told me) he felt reassured about me being a good person to benefit from the operation. So, a few weeks later, I checked in. It was an enormously luxurious place. They had one-to-one nursing, i.e. as many nurses as there were patients, although you might not have had the same nurse all through the day. The nurses were all from New Zealand, pleasant and highly efficient. Needless to say, I had a room of my own, with a direct private telephone line – not through an exchange. I could have visitors at any time – a few of my friends in London actually came to see me. The food was superb, as in a top-class restaurant. Each morning a woman from the catering staff came in with a printed menu for lunch and supper. If I did not find on it anything to my liking, they told me, I only needed to say so and the chef would come up in person to discuss my meals with me. One day, I remember, I had Lobster Thermidor for lunch and grilled salmon in the evening. I was given a daily bath by two young nurses (who always politely apologized when they had to touch my genitals). After two days or so I was made to walk up and down the corridor with the assistance of a nurse, a day or two later I graduated to negotiating the stairs. I was told my operation had lasted four and a half hours, that my heart had been deliberately stopped at one point and then restarted. I am sure they must have given me painkillers during my stay there, without my knowing it, perhaps in my drinking water, because I felt no pain at all while I was there, although I had a scar all the way down my chest and down my left leg from my thigh to my ankle. The wires round my breastbone, where they bound it together again after sawing it apart, still show clearly through my skin.

Recovery at home, after my discharge, took quite a while. I had to walk a little every day, at first with a stick and very slowly, and I discovered with some surprise that our village, which I had always regarded as being entirely flat, had so many 'hills'. But after a few weeks my strength returned and I felt better than I had done before my heart attack. Naturally, this brush with one's mortality makes one think.

The following year, while we were in Florida, I had an attack of atrial fibrillations one morning and was taken to hospital in Naples. There they implanted a pacemaker below my left shoulder; this has to be inspected and tested at my local Pacemaker Clinic every few months. It also means that I cannot go through the magnetic security gates at airports but must be manually examined, and that I must use my mobile phone only on my right ear. These are not problems that worry me.

The doctors attributed the fact that I took the operation so well to my regular skiing until age 72. (In fact, I have often regretted that, on the advice of my cardiologist, I gave it up then.)

These health problems, fortunately, did not greatly affect my professional work. In fact, 1997 saw the publication of a major new biography of Albert Einstein – first in the USA, then in Britain, and a year later as a paperback. That same year, 1997 – after a two-year gap without awards – brought me an honorary membership of the European 'Franz Kafka' Circle, an honorary membership of the Jednota tlumočníků a překladatelů, the Czech translators' union, together with a Festschrift sponsored by them for my eightieth birthday, the Prize of the Masaryk Academy of Arts, and – the highest honour of all – the Medal of Merit [Medaile Za zásluhy], second class, presented to me on 28 October, the National Day, by President Václav Havel.

This was a wonderful ceremony in the ancient Vladislav Hall of the Castle, preceded by the national anthem and fanfares, with the names of the recipients – about thirty of them, read out, with a brief citation, by the Head of the President's Office. Most of the government and the diplomatic corps were present, as well as just one accompanying person for each recipient. In my case this was our son Richard, who had also driven me there from our hotel. The ceremony was followed by a reception in the splendid 'representational rooms' of the presidential wing of the Castle. I remember speaking to Václav Klaus, then the premier and now the president (his wife dragged me along to meet him), to Petr Pithart, the Speaker of the Senate, and to Jan Halas, the poet's younger son, whom I had met before.

Earlier that year, on my eightieth birthday in May, we decided to have a slap-up party – with little work for Mary and none for myself. We got a catering firm that we knew of to do everything – set up a big marquee on our lawn, provide all the food and drink, as well as tables, chairs, plates, glasses and cutlery, serve starters and drinks on our patio, later serve the food and drink in the marquee, including the champagne for the toasts. We had all my and Mary's family and relations – my brother and his family came from Germany, our son and his (then) fiancée came from the Czech Republic – as well as more than half a dozen school friends of mine, including one who came from Holland. There were forty of us in all. Halfway through our meal in the marquee we heard some hurdy-gurdy music outside. We discovered that our daughter Margaret had hired a barrel-organ player she had met at some folk music festival to come and play just outside our garden fence. We later made him come into our garden, much to the joy of the half-dozen children among our guests.

We had a similar event in June 2002, our diamond wedding, sixty years of marriage. This time it was not in our garden, but – to make things easier still – in a restored stone barn some seven or eight miles from us. We had just under fifty guests, including six of my prewar Prague friends.

Ever since the late 1980s I have been involved in a major translation project for Oxford University Press – a huge scholarly history of the Second World War in ultimately twelve volumes, each volume running to 800 or 1000 pages. On the first two volumes of Germany and the Second World War I was merely one of a team of four translators; from Volume 3 onward, for the next four volumes, I was not only one of the four translators but also the 'translation co-ordinator', which meant that I had to check the translations of my colleagues and ensure that they harmonized in usage of military and other terms. It was a big job. When the latest volume came along – by which time I was eighty-three – I took on a major part of the translation but declined to be the co-ordinator; instead I found them a colleague willing to take on this task. This volume is now in preparation.

Only one of the more than 150 books I have translated became a best-seller. This was *The Man in the Ice*, published in 1994 in England and the following year in New York – not a literary work but the account of the discovery in an Alpine glacier of the well-preserved remains of a pre-historic hunter. It was a fascinating story, even more interesting to me because I knew the area in the Tyrol where the find was made. The book remained on the bestseller list for some time, and it is the only one of my translations that sold so well that the 'royalty clause' in my translation contract came into effect. (The customary arrangement is that royalties become payable only once they exceed the translation fee paid to the translator.) I am happy to say that twelve years after publication I still get a small royalty cheque every year.

1997 saw the publication of what – along with the *Correspondence between Richard Strauss and Hugo von Hofmannsthal* – is probably the most 'important' book I have translated. It was a biography and discussion of the philosophy of Martin Heidegger, titled *Martin Heidegger: Between Good and Evil*. It was possibly also the most difficult book I ever tackled and the one that involved an enormous amount of library research. But it was very widely reviewed on both sides of the Atlantic, usually over several pages.

In the mid-nineties a Czech friend of mine, Ivana Bozděchová, asked me to read, and perhaps criticize, her volume of translations of the Irish poet Desmond Egan. I was very much impressed by her handling of poetic language and – always something of an adventurer – suggested to her that we translate a selection of Seamus Heaney's recent poetry into Czech. This appeared in 1998 under the title *Jasanová hůl*, published by Volvox-Globator in Prague, with an introduction by Miroslav Holub. Heaney's poetry is enormously difficult to translate and, although I believe that we succeeded as well as anyone could expect, reception of the volume was mixed. Holub liked our translations, Jana Štroblová found fault with them. Undeterred we decided to translate a very different poet next – Wendy Cope. Translating her was, obviously, much more fun than wrestling with Seamus Heaney, and our (attractively produced) little volume *Zatracený chlapi*, was published by DITA in Prague in 1999. The following year the British Council invited Wendy Cope to give readings in Prague, Olomouc and Brno. Wendy had not been to Prague before: Ivana and I showed her the sights and, by arrangement with the British Council, shared her readings with her. After a well-attended reading in Prague the British Council provided its car and (very pleasant) driver to take us to Olomouc, where we had a joint reading at the university – my son and daughter-in-law had come over for it from Vsetín and we all had a jolly evening meal at a restaurant there afterwards. We stayed at a local hotel, at British Council expense, and the next day went to Brno for the final reading before returning to Prague. It was an enjoyable and successful tour and, although the publishers sent along their entire stock, the demand exceeded the supply. We were glad that Wendy Cope was able to convince herself that our Czech translations went down very well with the audience.

In 1999, when I went to the Památník národního písemnictví, the Czech national literary archive, to deposit my correspondence with

Jaroslav Seifert there, they invited me, to my great amazement, to deposit my entire literary archive with them. It was, of course, a great honour and I accepted eagerly, especially as Mary had been worrying about what would happen to all my papers if, as is statistically probable, I died first. In 2000 therefore, the transfer was arranged through the Czech Ministry of Foreign Affairs; the Czech embassy in London sent a 'diplomatic' van – normally used to transport the belongings of newly appointed or recalled diplomats – to our place in Sonning Common, along with two strong young men from the embassy staff, one of whom turned out to be the son of a poet whom I had met many years previously and some of whose poems I had translated. They loaded up the forty-odd cartons and drove them to London. For a while they were kept at the embassy (the vehicle not being available at the time), but eventually they were taken to Prague and they are now in the stage of being 'processed'. My name now appears on a large tablet in the entrance to the Strahov archives, along with some much more famous names than mine, and just a few names before that of Václav Havel.

Except for wintering in Florida – which Mary regards as 'her holiday' – she had only made three short trips abroad over the past twenty years or so. All of these were to the Czech Republic: in 1983 to visit our son in Šilheřovice, his first job abroad, in 1987 to Prague, when I received my Medal of Merit from President Havel, and again to Prague in 1998, when Richard and Hana got married there at the Old Town Hall. But there was one venue that she had long dreamed of visiting – the Norwegian coastline. So when, early in 2001 and almost by accident, I discovered an agency on the internet, called Medical Travel, which offered cruises along the Norwegian coast on ships with special facilities for handicapped passengers, we followed this up and eventually booked an eleven-day cruise from Bergen in June, all the way past the northern tip of Norway to Kirkenes, and back. This proved absolutely wonderful and exceeded our expectations. Except for our first day we had wonderful weather throughout, the scenery, which slowly sailed past the window on the non-smoker deck, where we sat, was spectacular, the midnight sun was a unique experience, the food was superb, our cabin – the Kong Harald had three special cabins for disabled passengers – was very comfortable, and the staff (or crew) were obliging and very pleasant. The ship stopped about thirty times each way – some of the stops quite short merely to load or unload supplies and serve local passengers, and others long enough to allow people to go ashore and sightsee. Myself, I got off at Trondheim, the ancient capital, at Tromsö, and at a very northerly stop to take a tourist bus to the North Cape, the northernmost point of the European continent. The 'trip of a lifetime' of the brochure was no exaggeration. We are very glad we took it while we were sufficiently mobile to do so.

'But I have promises to keep
And miles to go before I sleep'

(Robert Frost)

This brings us to the end of this story. In the course of 2001 and 2002 seven translated books of mine were published, though admittedly one of them is only a small bibliophile publication of 16 pages, on the 100th anniversary of František Halas's birth. Another was a selection of the work of Jan Skácel (with an introduction by Ivan Klíma).

Among my prose translations during these past few years the one I am proudest of is Arnošt Lustig's *Lovely Green Eyes*. This is a wonderful book, powerful and at the same time sensitive, set (like nearly all of Lustig's novels) against a Holocaust background. It was published in England by Harvill Press and, almost simultaneously, in America by Arcade Publishing. It is not a mass appeal book, but it had some wonderful reviews – one of them actually suggesting that Lustig should be given the next Nobel Prize for Literature. Rather exasperatingly, Lustig kept rewriting the book while I was already translating it, cutting out big chunks and rearranging the chapters – and, in consultation with the British publisher, I did some more cutting and rearranging. In the course of this far from smooth collaboration Arnošt and I became good friends and I was to translate another book of his before long.

2001 also brought me three major prizes – the John Sykes Memorial Award for Excellence, presented to me by the British Institute of Translation and Interpreting, the Jan Masaryk 'Gratias agit' Award, handed to me at the Czernin Palace in Prague by Deputy Premier and Foreign Minister Jan Kavan, and the Premia Bohemica Prize awarded to me by the Obec spisovatelů, the Czech Writer's Union. I did not think that this kind of annus mirabilis would happen to me again. In point of fact, however, I received three more translation prizes during the first six months of 2002 – the Aurora Borealis Prize for Outstanding Translation of Fiction Literature and, astonishingly, the Aurora Borealis Prize for

Outstanding Translation of Non-Fiction Literature. Both these prizes are awarded by FIT, the International Federation of Translators, at its triennial Congress, this time (in my absence) in Vancouver. These two prizes have never before been awarded to the same translator in the same year. But as each prize has its own jury of five persons, whose deliberations are secret and not known to each other, I can be sure that there was no collusion. And the third prize in 2002 was the Karel Hynek Mácha prize of the Masaryk Academy of Art in Prague.

My translation work and publication of my translations continued in 2003. At the very beginning of the year my translation of an interesting biography of Franz Kafka (written in German by Klaus Wagenbach) appeared in England (Haus Publishers) and in America (Harvard University Press), as well as an amusing little book by Arnošt Lustig, *The Breviary of F. Vondráček*. In the spring, about a year after its first publication, there appeared a paperback edition of Lustig's *Lovely Green Eyes*. This new edition (by Vintage Press) was highly successful: one of Britain's biggest bookseller chains, W. H. Smith, chose it as its 'Book of the Month' for April, exhibiting it on little tables in all their shops. The book's American publishers, Arcade, entered it for the Pulitzer Prize, but unfortunately it did not get into the final shortlist. In England, however, it got into the five finalists for the '*Jewish Quarterly* Wingate Prize' and into the seven finalists (out of 70 contenders) for the Weidenfeld Translated Literature Prize. But it failed to win either. Even so, some 30,000 copies were sold – a considerable success for a book that isn't exactly light or entertaining reading.

2003 saw the publication, in the Czech Republic, of an attractive bilingual edition of Vítězslav Nezval's cycle *Edison*. Translation of Nezval's rhymed couplets, with moreover a lot of fun-rhymes, was technically difficult, but I enjoyed the challenge and I think made quite a good job of it.

To my great surprise I even had a theatrical success in September 2003. An American writer, Emily Solomon, had produced a dramatized version of my translation of Karel Čapek's *War with the Newts* and this was staged – read rather than fully acted – at the Kennedy Center in Washington DC within the From Page to Stage Festival – New Plays. It was performed by the Washington Stage Guild, a company well known for its performances of G.B. Shaw's plays. A radio adaptation of the same book was broadcast twice by the BBC and a film adaptation is presently being worked on.

I am particularly pleased that these *Memoirs*, translated by Ivana Bozděchová, were published in Prague in 2004 by the prestigious Karolinum, the publishing house of Charles University, Prague. The same publisher also, as the 'Rector's New Year Present' – i.e. as a private, non-commercial publication – brought out a small (23-page) volume of Jaroslav Seifert's poems, bilingually, with my English translations.

Early in 2004 another small volume was published in the Czech Republic – a series of 14 of my own poems about Prague, also bilingually, with Czech translations mainly by Ivana Bozděchová. It may even be regarded as a trilingual publication, since it contains two of my earliest poems about Prague, then still written in German.

Publication is also due, I hope before too long, in Slovakia, of a volume of poems for children by Miroslav Válek.

In June 2004 another novel by Arnošt Lustig, *Waiting for Leah*, came out in my translation, again with Harvill Press. To mark the 150th anniversary of the birth of Leoš Janáček a translation of *On an Overgrown Path*, a biography of the composer by the Czech author Kožík was due to appear, but there was a little hold-up and it did not appear until 2006. There was a launch event for it in Prague – even though it was an English book – in a fine old building on Kampa island, now a Museum of Medieval Handicrafts. About seventy people turned up for the event. A few months later the book was again launched at the Czech embassy in London in the presence of over 50 guests.

2007 will, it is hoped, see the publication of Volume 7 of *Germany and the Second World War* (where I am just one of four translators). And finally – or what may seem 'finally' from when I am writing this now – there will be a multimedia collection of Jaroslav Seifert's poetry, a bilingual book with a CD on which several of Seifert's poems are spoken by the Czech actor Chudík.

2007 may also see the publication of a volume of poems by Jaromír Hořec (the Czech publisher is still seeking a sponsor) and of a long and rather fine historical novel, *Cleopatra*, by Vlasta Brtníková. A bilingual edition of Zdeněk Vaníček's humorous stories has already appeared in the Czech Republic.

In the late autumn of 2006 a volume of poems by the leading Slovak poet, Milan Rúfus, appeared in the United States. The translations are by me (more than half of them) and by Viera and John Sutherland-Smith.

In the summer of 2007 a trilingual volume of the Lachian poetry of

Óndra Lysohorsky (English – Lachian – Czech) with my English trans-lations and a long essay by me on the poet will appear in Prague, at the publishing house of the Czech Academy of Sciences.

Despite this flurry of publications 2004 was a bad year for me in terms of health. In May, after weeks of considerable pain, I had a total hip replacement and recovered from it surprisingly fast. However, in November I had to go into hospital for a week with an acute urinary problem. After several uncomfortable, rather than painful, weeks with a catheter I had a prostate resection in mid-January 2005 and am by now, relatively speaking, as good as new. I sincerely hope I won't see the inside of a hospital again for a long time. These unpleasant aspects of 2004 were, however, offset by two festive book launches, jointly of the Czech edition of my Memoirs, *Loňské sněhy* [*Snows of Yesteryear*] and of *Golden City / Zlaté město*, my volume of poems about Prague. The first of these launches took place at the Czech Embassy in London, with speeches by the ambassador and by James Naughton, the professor of Czech at Oxford University. Zdena Tomínová, a well-known signatory of the Charta 77, read some of my poetry in Czech and English (and even an early one in German). I had invited many of my friends and it was a rather splendid affair. A few months later a similar launch, again of both books, took place in Prague, at the Cultural Department of the Jewish Council in Prague. Professor Martin Hilský gave an (over-generous) laudatio and an actor of the National Theatre read several of the poems in Czech. My son Richard and his wife Hana had come to Prague for the occasion. Apart from my health problems 2004 may therefore be said to have been an annus mirabilis.

Two young Slovak Jews succeeded, against all odds, in escaping from the Auschwitz extermination camp during the war. A few more had managed to escape before them, but the escape of these two was signif-icant because they carried with them detailed documentary evidence of what was happening at Auschwitz. This evidence they managed to get into Switzerland and into the hands of the British and Americans. One of the two men, Alfred Wetzler, wrote a book about the conditions at Auschwitz, about their adventurous escape and about the difficulties they encountered upon their return in making people believe in the mass murder that was taking place there. This book, which I translated largely on emotional grounds, because I believe that the memory of the Holocaust should be kept alive, will appear in the spring of 2007 under the title *Escape from Hell*, together with the actual text of the 'Auschwitz protocol' and with a preface by Sir Martin Gilbert.

During the late months of 2005 and January 2006 I also translated a German book, printed in the now obsolete 'Gothic' or 'Black Letter' font, titled *Call of the Caravan*, about some desert exploration in the years immediately preceding the Second World War. I was commissioned to make this translation by the son of the author, who is a member of the Swedish parliament and whose children no longer speak German; it is not certain yet whether it will be taken up by a publisher. In the course of 2006, I also translated a book by Dieter Senghaas, the founder and director of the Frankfurt Institute of Peace Research. This is due to appear in 2007.

As I said in my acceptance speech at a recent prize-giving, I have no intention of stopping working. I enjoy literary translation, I enjoy the intellectual, artistic and linguistic challenge. No other activity, and certainly not leisure, would give me the same satisfaction. It would be nice to bring the total of my translated books up to the round figure of 160 – but time will tell.

Chronology

1917
born 13 May in Prague
1923
starts primary school in Vladislavova
1927
starts secondary school in Štěpánská
1935
graduates from secondary school, starts study of
chemistry at German University
1937
German translations of contemporary Czech poetry, published in
Prager Presse; joins the left-wing literary group *Blok*: own poems
and translations in the quarterly *U*; contacts with Josef Hora,
František Halas, Óndra Lysohorsky; beginning of systematic
translation of Lysohorsky's poetry
1938
relocates to England, studies at University College London
1939
in spring last meeting with his mother; in September
joins BBC Monitoring Service
1940
external student (Russian language and literature)
at University of London
1942
marriage to Mary Harman
1943
collaboration with Karel Brušák, Pavel Tigrid and Valter Berger
on *Review-42* (to *Review-46*); regular translations of poetry and
book reviews in *Central European Observer*
1944
occasional translations for Czechoslovak government in exile,
acquaintance with Jiří Mucha, Eduard Goldstücker and Viktor Fischl
1945
publication of his first book, *Modern Czech Poetry* and his first prose

book, *The Problems of Lieutenant Knap* by Jiří Mucha; move to
London and assumption of the London editorial office of *Review-45*

1947

birth of daughter Margaret on 21 April

1951

birth of son Richard on 9 May

1956

publication of first translation from German; beginning of regular
work for Harrap publishing house; first post-war visit to Prague
(with family), meeting with brother Jan and his family

1961

publication of his 'most important' book, *The Correspondence
between Richard Strauss and Hugo von Hofmannsthal*
(with Hanns Hammelmann)

1962

two months' 'attachment' to Russian Section of BBC European
Service, promotion to Chief Editor

1964

first visit to America

1970

begins to write his own poetry in English;
publication in literary journals

1971

Schlegel -Tieck Prize for best translation
from German during previous year

1976

publication of first volume of his poetry, *Wish You Were Here*

1977

retirement from BBC; lecture tour of American universities;
beginning of regular visits to Prague

1978

publication of *The Plague Column* by Jaroslav Seifert

1983

publication of *An Umbrella from Piccadilly* by Jaroslav Seifert; first
meeting with Miroslav Holub at Cambridge Poetry Festival

1984

election as Fellow of the Royal Society of Literature

1985

Cyril and Methodius Order (1st class), Bulgaria

1986

publication of *The Selected Poetry of Jaroslav Seifert* simultaneously in
London and New York; Gold Medal with Ribbon of the Czechoslovak
Society for International Relations; *Anamnéza*, a selection
of his poems in Czech translation by Zlata Kufnerová

1987

European Poetry Translation Prize

1989

Honorary degree (Dr.h.c.phil.) from Palacký University, Olomouc

1990

Officer's Cross of the Order of Merit of the Federal German Republic

1996

Joint Prize of the Macedonian Writers' Union
and Macedonian Translators' Union

1997

Quadruple bypass operation, following a slight heart attack

1997

Medal of Merit (2nd class) of the Czech Republic,
from President Havel on 28 October

1999

Deposition of his papers at the Czech Literary Archive in Prague;
Jan Masaryk Gratias agit award (from Ministry of Foreign
Affairs of the Czech Republic); Premia Bohemica Prize
from the Czech Writers' Guild

2001

Aurora Borealis Prize for Outstanding Translation of Fiction
and Aurora Borealis Prize for Outstanding Translation
of Non-Fiction (from International Federation of
Translators); Karel Hynek Mácha Prize from
Masaryk Academy of Arts

2004

Publication of *Loňské sněhy*, his memoirs in Czech translation
by Ivana Bozděchová; publication of *Golden City / Zlaté město*,
a collection of his poems about Prague, bilingually
(Czech translation chiefly by Ivana Bozděchová)

2004

Hip replacement operation

2005

Prostate resection

2006
In Prague in September: festive launch, at the Museum of Medieval
Handicrafts with about 70 guests present, of *Encounters with Leoš
Janáček.* In November an 'English launch' hosted by the Czech
embassy in London, with a little over 50 guests. Also, in
America, publication of *And That's The Truth: Poems
by Milan Rúfus*

Complete Bibliography

BOOKS TRANSLATED FROM GERMAN

OFF LIMITS by Hans Habe; Harrap, London 1956; Frederick Fell, New York 1956; World Distributors, Manchester (paperback) 1958

ALL MY SINS by Hans Habe; Harrap, London 1958

AGENT OF THE DEVIL by Hans Habe; Harrap, London 1958; [as THE DEVIL'S AGENT] Frederick Fell, New York 1958; Transworld Publications, Manchester (paperback) 1959; New English Library 1968; White Lion Publishers 1973

THE NEW FACE OF CHINA by Peter Schmidt; Harrap, London 1958

EUROPE FROM THE AIR by Emil Egli; Harrap, London 1959

INDIA: MIRAGE AND REALITY by Peter Schmidt; Harrap, London 1961

MEN AND MOLECULES by Carl R. Theiler; Harrap, London 1960; Dodd, Mead Co., New York 1962

THE CORRESPONDENCE BETWEEN RICHARD STRAUSS AND HUGO VON HOFMANNSTHAL (in collaboration with H. A. Hammelmann); Collins, London 1961 [as A WORKING FRIENDSHIP, THE CORRESPONDENCE BETWEEN RICHARD STRAUSS AND HUGO VON HOFMANNSTHAL) Random House, New York 1961; Vienna House, New York (paperback) 1961; Cambridge University Press (paperback) 1974

INVASION: THEY'RE COMING! by Paul Carell; Harrap, London 1962; Dutton Co., New York 1963; Transworld Publications, Manchester (paperback) 1963; Bantam Books, New York (paperback) 1964

PHYSICS FOR YOU AND ME by Wilhelm W. Westphal; Harrap, London 1962; [as FUN WITH PHYSICS] Four Square Books, London (paperback) 1964; [as PHYSICS CAN BE FUN] Hawthorn Books Inc., New York 1965

NO OTHER WAY by Herbert L. Schrader; Harrap, London 1963; David McKay, New York 1964

MERCHANTS MAKE HISTORY by Ernst Samhaber; Harrap, London 1963; John Day, New York 1964

HITLER'S WAR ON RUSSIA by Paul Carell; Harrap, London 1964; [as HITLER MOVES EAST 1941-1943] Little Brown, Boston 1965; Corgi Books, London (paperback) 1966; reprinted 1967; [as HITLER MOVES EAST 1941-1943] Bantam Books, New York (p/b) 1966; again as Vol. 1 of HITLER'S WAR ON RUSSIA (HITLER MOVES EAST) Corgi Books, London (p/b) 1971; Fedorowicz, Canada (p/b) 1996

A SHORT TEXTBOOK OF PHYSICS by Wilhelm W. Westphal; Springer-Verlag, Heidelberg, Berlin, New York 1968

MEXICO by H. Leuenberger and A. Annaheim; Harrap, London 1968

THE PUPPET THEATRE OF THE MODERN WORLD [the German half of the book]; Harrap, London 1966

THE AEGEAN WORLD by Dr. H. Nawrat; Kümmerly + Frey, Berne 1969

SPITSBERGEN by Julius Budel and Walter Imber; Kümmerly + Frey, Berne 1969

THE SAHARA by René Gardi [in collaboration with Henry Fox]; Harrap, London 1969

SCORCHED EARTH by Paul Carell; Harrap, London 1970; Little Brown. Boston 1970; as Vol. 2 of HITLER'S WAR ON RUSSIA (SCORCHED EARTH); Corgi Books, London (paperback) 1971

THE CAMARGUE by Karl Weber and Lukas Hoffmann; Kümmerly + Frey, Berne 1970; Harrap, London 1971

ALASKA by Heinrich Gohl; Kümmerly + Frey, Berne 1970

THE SECRET CONFERENCES OF DR. GOEBBELS 1939-43 by Willi A. Boelcke (ed.); Weidenfeld, London 1970; Dutton Co., New York 1970

CHINESE FOLKTALES; G. Bell and Sons, London 1971

MAYERLING – THE FACTS BEHIND THE LEGEND by Fritz Judtmann; Harrap, London 1971

SELECTED POEMS BY ONDRA LYSOHORSKY; Cape Editions, London 1971; Grossman Publishers Inc., New York 1971

I SAW SIBERIA by Hugo Portisch; [in collaboration with Henry Fox] Harrap, London 1972; Dutton Co., New York 1972

TO UNPLUMBED DEPTHS by Hans Hass; Harrap, London 1972; [as CHALLENGING THE DEEP] William Morrow & Co., Inc., New York 1973

THE AUSTRIAN EXAMPLE by Kurt Waldheim; Weidenfeld, London 1972

UNDERSEAS POSSESSIONS: SELECTED POEMS BY HANS-JÜRGEN HEISE; Oleander Press, Stoughton, Wisconsin 1972

WITH THE VOLUME TURNED DOWN & OTHER POEMS BY REINER KUNZE; London Magazine Editions, London 1973

THE MAFIA by Henner Hess; D.C. Heath, Farnborough 1973; C. Hurst, London, 1998; (paperback) 1998

THE FOREST by W. Kümmerly (ed.); Kümmerly + Frey, Berne 1973; Robert B. Luce, Washington DC 1973

THREE FACES OF MARXISM by Wolfgang Leonhardt; Holt, Reinhart & Winston, New York 1974

ICELAND by F.K. v. Linden and H. Weyer; [in collaboration with Lux Furtmüller] Almenna Bokafelagid, Reykjavik 1974

GRAND CANYON by E.A. Heiniger; Kümmerly + Frey, Berne 1974

SOCIALIST CRIMINOLOGY by E. Buchholz et al.; D.C. Heath, Farnborough 1974

GERMANY FACETS: Catalogue of the German Book Exhibition in Britain and Ireland, 1974

THE DELIAN ARETALOGY OF SARAPIS by H. Engelmann; E.J. Brill, Leyden 1975

INDIA by Hans Bosch et al.; Kümmerly + Frey, Berne 1976

CEYLON by Robert Hobel; Kümmerly + Frey, Berne 1976

BALI by Robert Hobel; Kümmerly + Frey, Berne 1976

THE SOUTHERN CORDILLERA REAL by R. Pecher and W. Schmiemann; Plata Publications, Chur 1976

STRAWBERRIES IN DECEMBER & OTHER POEMS BY HANS-DIETER SCHÄFER; Carcanet Press, Cheadle 1976

TIBETAN SACRED ART by Detlev Ingo Lauf; Shambhala, Berkeley & London 1976

CONTEMPORARY GERMAN POETRY; Oleander Press, New York & Cambridge 1976

SELECTED POEMS BY ROSE AUSLÄNDER; London Magazine Editions, London 1977

THE LOVELY YEARS by Reiner Kunze; Sidgwick & Jackson, London 1978

A EUROPEAN PAST: Memoirs by Prince Clary; Weidenfeld, London 1978; St.Martin's Press, New York 1978

WHITHER AFRICA? by Heinz-Dietrich Ortlieb; Interfrom, Zurich 1978

GROWTH FOR ALL by Jürgen Todenhöfer; v. Hase & Koehler, Mainz 1979

THE MEANING OF HITLER by Sebastian Haffner; Weidenfeld, London 1979; Phoenix (paperback) 1997, reprinted 2000

WOUNDED NO DOUBT: SELECTED POEMS BY RUDOLF LANGER; Menard Press, London 1979

SWITZERLAND by Jeanneret, Imber and Auf der Maur; Kümmerly + Frey, Berne 1979

THE WORLD POCKET ATLAS; Kümmerly + Frey, Berne 1979

SWEDEN by W. Imber and W. Tietze; Kümmerly + Frey, Berne 1979

NORWAY by W. Imber and W. Tietze; Cappelen, Oslo 1980

ECONOMY AND DEVELOPMENT by J. Thesing (ed.); 1980

THE RISE AND FALL OF PRUSSIA by Sebastian Haffner; Weidenfeld, London 1980

WITHOUT REMISSION: SELECTED POEMS BY WALTER HELMUT FRITZ; Menard Press, London 1981

THE MARX-ENGELS CORRESPONDENCE: THE PERSONAL LETTERS 1844-1877, a selection edited by K. Raddatz; Weidenfeld, London 1981; Little Brown, Boston 1982

DENMARK by W. Imber and P. Stokholm; Kümmerly + Frey, Berne 1981

THE EC'S GENERALIZED SYSTEM OF TARIFF PREFERENCES; 1981

EUROPEAN PORCELAIN by P.W. Meister and H. Reber; Phaidon Press, Oxford 1983; Cornell University Press 1983

ELECTION CAMPAIGNS by Peter Radunski; 1983

THE AGE OF IDEOLOGIES by Karl Dietrich Bracher; Weidenfeld, London 1984; St.Martin's Press, New York, 1984; Methuen, London (paperback) 1985

RETURN TO TIBET by Heinrich Harrer; Weidenfeld, London 1984; Penguin Books (paperback) 1985; Phoenix (paperback) 2000

NOT MARKED ON THE MAP: SELECTED POEMS BY HANNS CIBULKA; Aquila, Isle of Skye 1985

GORBACHEV: THE PATH TO POWER by Christian Schmidt-Häuer; [with Christ Romberg] I.B. Tauris, London 1986

WITTGENSTEIN'S NEPHEW by Thomas Bernhard; Quartet Publications, London 1986

GUSTAV KLIMT: WOMEN, with an essay by Angelica Bäumer; Weidenfeld, London 1986

CUTTING TIMBER by Thomas Bernhard; Quartet Publications, London 1987; Vintage (paperback) 1993

GUSTAV KLIMT: LANDSCAPES, with an essay by Johannes Dobai and a biography of Gustav Klimt; Weidenfeld, London 1988

SCHOPENHAUER AND THE WILD YEARS OF PHILOSOPHY by Rüdiger Safranski; Weidenfeld 1989; Harvard University Press 1990, 1991

OLD MASTERS by Thomas Bernhard; Quartet Publications, London 1989; University of Chicago Press, 1991; (Phoenix Fiction paperback) University of Chicago Press, 1992

JUSTICE NOT VENGEANCE by Simon Wiesenthal; Weidenfeld, London 1989; Grove Weidenfeld, New York 1989; Mandarin (paperback) 1990

GERMANY AND THE SECOND WORLD WAR, Vol. 1 (The Build-up of Aggression); [Part II] Clarendon Press, Oxford 1990

GERMANY AND THE SECOND WORLD WAR, Vol. 2 (Germany's Initial Conquests in Europe); [Parts III, VI, IX] Clarendon Press, Oxford 1991

THE CHEAP-EATERS by Thomas Bernhard; Quartet Publications, London 1991

YES by Thomas Bernhard; Quartet Publications, London 1991; University of Chicago Press (paperback), 1992

THE END OF THE NOVEL by Michael Krüger; Quartet Publications, London 1991; Braziller, New York, 1992

THE MAN IN THE ICE by Konrad Spindler; Weidenfeld, London 1994; (paperback) 1995, 1996, 2001

STRIKING THE BALANCE: THE HISTORY OF THE OPPENHEIM BANK; Weidenfeld, London 1995

GERMANY AND THE SECOND WORLD WAR, Vol. 3; (The Mediterranean, South-East Europe, and North Africa 1939-1941) [Part I] Clarendon Press, Oxford 1995

GERMANY AND THE SECOND WORLD WAR, Vol. 4; Clarendon Press, Oxford, 1999

GERMANY AND THE SECOND WORLD WAR, Vol. 5/1; Clarendon Press, Oxford, 2000

SELECTED POEMS BY HEINZ PIONTEK; Forest Books, London 1994

GERMANY AND THE SECOND WORLD WAR, Vol. 6; Clarendon Press, Oxford, 2001

ALBERT EINSTEIN: A BIOGRAPHY, by Albrecht Fölsing; Viking (USA), New York, 1997; Viking (UK), London, 1997; Penguin (paperback), London 1998

MARTIN HEIDEGGER: BETWEEN GOOD AND EVIL, by Rüdiger Safranski, Harvard University Press, Cambridge, Mass., 1998; London; (paperback) Harvard University Press, 1999

CODE BREAKING, by Rudolf Kippenhahn; Overlook Press, Woodstock & New York, 1999; Constable, London 1999

THE GERMAN CENTURY, by Prof. Stürmer; Endeavour Group (UK), 1999

THE WAGNERS, by Nike Wagner; (with Michael Downes), Weidenfeld & Nicolson, 2000; Princeton University Press, 2001

THE AUTHOR OF HIMSELF: THE LIFE OF MARCEL REICH-RANICKI; Weidenfeld & Nicolson, 2001; London, Phoenix (paperback), 2002

SPEER: THE FINAL VERDICT, by Joachim Fest; (with Alexandra Dring), Weidenfeld & Nicolson, 2001

KAFKA, by Klaus Wagenbach; Harvard University Press, Cambridge, MA, 2003; Haus Publishing (paperback), London, 2003

GERMANY AND THE SECOND WORLD WAR, Vol. 7; Clarendon Press, Oxford, [in preparation for 2007]

ON PERPETUAL PEACE by Dieter Senghaas; Berghahn Books, Oxford, 2007

GERMANY AND THE SECOND WORLD WAR, Vol. 9/1; Clarendon Press, Oxford [in preparation for 2007]

BOOKS TRANSLATED FROM CZECH

MODERN CZECH POETRY in collaboration with J.K. Montgomery; Allen & Unwin, London 1945

THE PROBLEMS OF LIEUTENANT KNAP by Jiří Mucha; Hogarth Press, London 1945

SCORCHED CROP by Jiří Mucha; Hogarth Press, London 1949

MISSING by Egon Hostovský; Secker & Warburg, London 1952; Viking Press, New York 1952; Bantam Books, New York (paperback) 1953

LIVING AND PARTLY LIVING by Jiří Mucha; Hogarth Press, London 1967; McGraw Hill, New York 1968

THREE CZECH POETS: NEZVAL, BARTUŠEK, HANZLÍK; Penguin Books 1970

THE AZTEC CALENDAR & OTHER POEMS BY ANTONÍN BARTUŠEK; Anvil Press, London 1975

THE PLAGUE COLUMN: POEMS BY JAROSLAV SEIFERT; Terra Nova Editions, London & Boston 1979

JAROSLAV SEIFERT: DVĚ BÁSNĚ / TWO POEMS / TWÅ DIKTET; English translation by Ewald Osers, Charta 77 Foundation, Stockholm 1981

AN UMBRELLA FROM PICCADILLY: POEMS BY JAROSLAV SEIFERT; London Magazine Editions, London 1983

IN LOVE WITH LIFE: an anthology of contemporary Czech poetry; Artia, Prague 1983

ON THE CONTRARY & OTHER POEMS BY MIROSLAV HOLUB; Bloodaxe Books, Newcastle-upon-Tyne 1984

WAR WITH THE NEWTS by Karel Čapek; Allen & Unwin, London (paperback) 1985; Picador/Pan (paperback) 1991; Catbird Press, USA (paperback) 1990

THE SELECTED POETRY OF JAROSLAV SEIFERT; Macmillan Publishing Co., New York 1986 and André Deutsch, London 1986; Collier Books (Macmillan) (paperback), New York 1990. THE POETRY OF JAROSLAV SEIFERT; expanded, updated and revised: Catbird Press, North Haven, CT, 1998

MY FIRST LOVES by Ivan Klíma; Chatto & Windus, London 1986; Harper & Row, New York, 1988; Penguin Books, London (p/b) 1989; W.W. Norton, New York (p/b) 1989

A SUMMER AFFAIR by Ivan Klíma; Chatto & Windus, London 1987; Penguin Books London (paperback) 1990; reprinted 1994

THE FLY & OTHER POEMS BY MIROSLAV HOLUB; Bloodaxe Books, Newcastle-upon-Tyne 1987; Dufour, New York, 1987

WOMEN; a book of photographs by Stanislav Tůma with poems by Jaroslav Seifert; GTP Amsterdam 1987

THE NEW CZECH POETRY: JAROSLAV ČEJKA, MICHAL ČERNÍK, KAREL SÝS; Bloodaxe Books, Newcastle-upon-Tyne 1988; Dufour, New York, 1988

THE HOUSE OF THE TRAGIC POET by Vladimír Janovic; Bloodaxe Books, Newcastle-upon-Tyne 1988; Dufour, New York, 1988

POEMS BEFORE & AFTER by Miroslav Holub; Bloodaxe Books, Newcastle-upon-Tyne 1990; simultaneously in paperback; Dufour, New York, 1988; expanded edition: Bloodaxe Books 2006

LOVE AND GARBAGE by Ivan Klíma; Chatto & Windus, London 1990; [second revised edition] 1990; Penguin Books London (paperback) 1991; Knopf, New York, 1992

JOSEF HANZLÍK: SELECTED POEMS; with Ian and Jarmila Milner; Bloodaxe Books, Newcastle-upon-Tyne 1993; Dufour, New York, 1993

PRAGA CAPUT REGNI [a photographic book of Prague, with poems by Jaroslav Seifert]; Flow East RV, Amsterdam 1995

SUPPOSED TO FLY: A SEQUENCE FROM PILSEN, CZECHOSLOVAKIA, by Miroslav Holub; Bloodaxe Books, Newcastle-upon-Tyne, 1996; Dufour Editions, USA, 1996

KOLYA by Zdeněk Svěrák; Headline Book Publishing, London, 1997

AMONG MEMORY'S RUINS: POEMS BY ZDENĚK VANÍČEK; Oasis Books, London 1999

AGED WOMEN by František Halas; Oasis Books, London, 2001

LOVELY GREEN EYES, by Arnošt Lustig; Harvill Press, London, 2002; Arcade Publishing, New York, 2002; Vintage (paperback), London 2003

BANNED MAN: SELECTED POEMS BY JAN SKÁCEL; Modrý Peter Publishing, Canada, 2002

EDISON, BY VÍTĚZSLAV NEZVAL; bilingual edition Czech/English; Dvořák, Czech Republic, 2003

THE BREVIARY OF A. VONDRÁČEK by Arnošt Lustig; Plast, Czech Republic, 2003

WHEREUPON HE WAS ARRESTED by Zdeněk Vaníček; Czech Republic, 2004

WAITING FOR LEAH by Arnošt Lustig; Harvill, London 2004

TO THE FOUR CORNERS OF THE EARTH by Zdeněk Vaníček; Prague 2005, 2nd edn. 2007

2005 [9 poems by Seifert], Universitas Carolina Pragensis, bilingual Czech and English, 23pp., unbound, soft covers [Rector's New Year present]

ENCOUNTERS WITH LEOŠ JANÁČEK by František Kožík; ELK, Prague, 2006

THE VRTBA GARDEN, a brochure of photographs with poems by Jaroslav Seifert and Jaroslav Vrchlický, Prague 2006

ÓNDRA LYSOHORSKY, a selection of his Lachian poetry with English and Czech translations and with an introductory essay by Ewald Osers; Academia, Prague 2007

BOOKS TRANSLATED FROM SLOVAK

THE GROUND BENEATH OUR FEET: SELECTED POEMS BY MIROSLAV VÁLEK; Modrý Peter Publishing, Levoča, Slovakia, and Bloodaxe Books, Newcastle-upon-Tyne 1996

HOW JACKO WAS LOST, Poems for Children by Miroslav Válek; Modrý Peter Publishing, Canada, 2003 [in preparation for 2007]

AND THAT'S THE TRUTH: POEMS BY MILAN RÚFUS with John Sutherland-Smith; Bolchazi-Carducci Publishers, Illinois, 2006

ESCAPE FROM HELL by Alfred Wetzler; Berghahn Books, Oxford, 2007

BOOKS TRANSLATED FROM BULGARIAN

THE ROAD TO FREEDOM: POEMS BY GEO MILEV; Sofia Press. Sofia 1983; Forest Books, London 1988

POEMS BY NIKOLA VAPTSAROV; Journeyman Press, London 1984; simultaneously in paperback

STOLEN FIRE: POEMS BY LYUBOMIR LEVCHEV; Forest Books, London 1986

FIRES OF THE SUNFLOWERS: POEMS BY IVAN DAVIDKOV; Forest Books, London 1988

BOOKS TRANSLATED FROM MACEDONIAN

FOOTPRINTS IN THE WIND: POEMS BY MATEJA MATEVSKI; Forest Books, London 1988

CONTEMPORARY MACEDONIAN POETRY; Kultura, Skopje & Forest Books, London 1991

BOOKS TRANSLATED FROM OTHER LANGUAGES

101 HAYRENS OF NAHAPET KUCHAK (13th century Armenian love poetry); Sovetakan Grogh, Erevan 1979

VOICES FROM ACROSS THE WATER (Translations from 12 languages); Prospice 16, Isle of Skye 1985

BOOKS TRANSLATED INTO CZECH

MY SPOKOJENÍ POZOROVATELÉ ZKÁZY [SELECTED POETRY OF GAVIN EWART] in collaboration with Zlata Kufnerová; Odeon, Prague 1992

JASANOVÁ HŮL [SELECTED POETRY BY SEAMUS HEANEY] in collaboration with Ivana Bozděchová; Volvox Globator, Prague, 1998

ZATRACENÝ CHLAPI [SELECTED POEMS BY WENDY COPE] in collaboration with Ivana Bozděchová; DITA Publishers, Prague 1999

First published in Great Britain by:

Elliott & Thompson Ltd
27 John Street
London WC1N 2BX

© Ewald Osers 2007

ISBN 1 904027 57 1 (10 digit)

ISBN 978 1 904027 57 7 (13 digit)

First edition

Book design by Brad Thompson

Printed and bound in Malta by Progress Press